Buddhist Teachings

The Art Of Letting Go

Inspired by the Talks of Ajahn Brahm

By Lorenzo da Costa

www.lorenzodacosta.com
www.soulace.co.uk

Purple Star Publishing

First Edition: 2014

Published by Purple Star Publishing
www.purplestarpublishing.com
info@purplestarpublishing.com

Cover Design by Jo Ward
Illustrations by Tim Lee

ISBN: 978-1-312-30180-1

DISCLAIMER

This book is compiled from a variety of sources over a number of years. Details can be found in the bibliography. The author is happy to correct any factual inaccuracies if duly informed. All opinions are those of the author only and do not necessarily reflect those of the publisher or Ajahn Brahm.

Please note that this text is not directly related to/authorized by Ajahn Brahm himself.

The information provided in this book is designed to provide helpful information on the subjects discussed. References are provided for informational purposes only and do not constitute endorsement or any websites or other sources. Readers should be aware that the websites listed in this book might change.

ACKNOWLEDGMENTS

I acknowledge with joy and pleasure the following people:

First of all I have to acknowledge and thank Ajahn Brahm who has become something of an Internet guru for me. Had I not felt inspired to collate and organise material from his You Tube talks, this book would never have come to be written.

My thanks to my various teachers within the 'Gurdjieff Work' in London with whom I have had an association for some twenty-five years. I feel an immense debt of gratitude to Robert Svoboda author of the amazing Aghora Trilogy. These books, which I have felt drawn to read in minute detail some six times in the last twenty years have given me specific help at interesting times in my own search.

I am immensely grateful to my contact with the Spiritualist Churches in London, whose mediums have given me concrete personal evidence of the survival 'on the other side' of my dear departed parents and evidence from my 'guides in spirit'. I now palpably feel their protection and guidance.

I wish to thank my GP colleague and author on a book on Spiritualism, Dr Ian Rubenstein for looking at the manuscript and writing a foreword.

And I wish to thank my publisher Jo Ward for her work on editing and arranging the manuscript.

And last but not least I wish to acknowledge the Great Guru to us all Google!

CONTENTS

SECTION ONE:
The Practice of Letting Go

1. Let go of doing hindsight

2. Let go of the idea of 'Why me?'

3. Let go of seeking for revenge

4. Let go of attachment to past suffering

5. Let go of grief at the passing of a loved one

6. Let go of labels and personas

7. Let go of the idea that we learn from the failures of the past

21. Let go of asking the world what it can never give you

22. Let go of the prisons of your life

23. Let go of conceit

24. Let go of the idea that you need more

25. Let go of the idea that you will do something about a "problem" at a future time

26. Let go of impatience

27. Let go of personal criticism about 'stuffing up'

28. Let go of the tendency to take criticism to heart

29. Let go of trying to be a control freak

30. Let go of the 'what's in it for me' attitude

31. Let go of wasting time on insoluble problems

32. Let go of indecision

33. Let go of anger

34. Let go of the idea that 'I can get what I want if I try hard enough'

35. Let go of the idea that 'life is hard'

SECTION TWO:
Buddhism, Hinduism, & Mystic Christianity

Part 1:
Buddhism & Hinduism A Personal Perspective 81

Part 2:
Seven Messages of The Bhagavad-Gita 91

Part 3:
Christianity Through Eastern Eyes 101

DEDICATION

This book is dedicated to the life and work of Ajahn Sumedho.

There are many in Europe and America who regard Ajahn Sumedho as a landmark figure and a founding father of the spread of The Dharma, the Buddhist teachings, in the West.

In a lifetime of spiritual searching, I have come across many who can talk the talk. Listening to Ajahn Sumedho at his Sunday afternoon Dhamma Talks at Amaravati Monastery in Hertfordshire, UK, in 2008 and 2009, I felt I was in the presence of a being that was walking the talk in the fullest possible sense. He exuded the aura of a being that had no past and no future, only the enormous largesse of the here and now. Simply being in his presence gave one what a hundred books could not. He exuded a quality of hope in the most sacred sense.

Had I not come across him, I suspect I would not have explored Buddhism in the way I have. Nor would I have come across Ajahn Brahm.

Both Ajahn Sumedho and Ajahn Brahm are disciples of the late Ajahn Chah.

FOREWORD

Dr Ian D Rubenstein, author of 'Consulting Spirit'

In this book, Dr da Costa presents his interpretation of the profound spiritual insights offered by one of the leading proponents of Modern Buddhism, Ajahn Brahm.

Dr da Costa addresses broad areas such as the need to let go of attachments and dealing with difficult emotions. Using discussion vignettes to explore the practical difficulties involved, his clear, no-nonsense writing style makes it a very easy read.

Dr da Costa is uniquely placed to offer us his insights. His background is eclectic. Growing up in India, he was exposed to many aspects of Eastern philosophy and spirituality from a young age. His education in medicine also gave him a firm foundation in the Western Rationalist method. He then came to the UK where he worked for many years as a UK primary care physician (GP), which offers the practitioner ample opportunity to observe the human condition.

Like many medical men, he has come to realise that much human suffering relates to the soul or psyche, the body often being merely an indicator of a deeper unease than the merely physical. This led him to pursue less conventional areas of healing. He now practices as an advisor on Complementary and Alternative Medicine and as a psycho-spiritual counselor.

In this book, Dr da Costa presents us not with just the wise words of Ajahn Brahm, and not with just some dry interpretation of abstruse ancient texts, but also offers us the insights of one who has witnessed the suffering of ordinary people and asked, "What can it mean?" and "How can I be of service?"

AUTHOR'S INTRODUCTION

Earlier life

I was born in 1955 in Kenya to Indian Catholic parents. At age 10, my family moved back into our ancestral home in Divar, Goa, which is where I grew up and went to the village school. I had no interest in philosophy or religion until the age of 18 when mystical experiences came to me out of the blue and utterly changed my life. My lifelong interest in eastern religions started at this time.

I joined Medical School in 1974 qualifying in 1980. In 1982 I came to Britain as an overseas doctor and obtained a qualification in Ear, Nose and Throat Surgery (Otolaryngology), a specialty I worked in for several years. I re took British undergraduate qualifications as a route out of hospital medicine into a career in General Medical Practice (Family Doctor). After a three year training program, I obtained my license, and in1995 joined a small practice looking after some 3500 patients in Richmond, a lovely part of London.

The DVD Set

In 2008 a series of unusual happenings led me to create an audiovisual lecture series called 'Going Nowhere – Journey into the Tao'. I submitted this in 2012 to Watkins Quarterly Review for assessment and Etan Ilfeld, compiler and producer of the Watkins 100 List, (Annual List of the 100 most Spiritually Influential Living Persons in the World). They were impressed and asked me to write a 500-word account of my personal journey. This article has appeared in the 2013 winter edition of the quarterly. He describes the product in the following way:

'This DVD set consists of lectures on Eastern spiritual practices and ideas. The lectures are clearly presented and well referenced with pointers to a number of popular authors on the subject.'

The article can be seen on my website, and the lecture on Medicine (40 minutes long) can be seen in full on my website as a You Tube clip. The wording of the article appears in Section Two of this book.

The Next Episode

In 2011, a series of strange and unexpected circumstances brought my conventional medical career to a crossroads.

I decided to take a sabbatical for at least a year to explore what I should do next.

My entire career had been spent doing conventional medicine as a day job and exploring spirituality, as a private interest. I was married to a spiritually oriented lady and we had no dependants. I had enough money to live on and so the future presented itself as something of a blank sheet.

Searching my heart and soul and asking my 'guides in spirit' for the way forward three events imprinted themselves on my psyche.

The first was an astrological consultation with a family friend Warren Kenton (Zev Ben Shimon Halevi) a teacher of the Kaballah. This was in 1985. He said that my chart showed that I would have a lifelong obsession with the esoteric and that I had the ability to become a priest-physician, which was quite rare. This would in fact be a karmic theme in my life story.

The second was astrological consultations with Masterjee, a Vedic Astrologer from Goa, India, a personal friend from 1980, who I met with socially on numerous occasions over the years. He said that my horoscope was curiously similar to that of Deepak Chopra, whom he knew, and that I was destined to pursue a similar line of work.

The third was a deep seated feeling that with my knowledge of the nuts and bolts of day to day practical medical practice and my feel for the unusual, the mysterious, the intangible and the esoteric, some sort of project or career to do with the medicine-metaphysics interface was what I was meant to do going forward. The practice of Medicine involves a continuous interaction with the world of information, as one has to continuously keep up to date. As part of the workings of an information-oriented mind I had acquired a vast amount of information about the world of the mysterious both related and unrelated to health and healing. I felt a desperate calling to find a career integrating the two.

In 2012 I commenced the liquidation of my career within conventional UK medicine and asked the General Medical Council to remove my name from their Register, this being necessary for medico legal reasons, in relation to the work I felt I would be doing going forwards.

Present Life

My present activities and interests embrace both Medicine and Spirituality both together and separately. I am also involved in London's Spiritualist scene, bringing me into contact with a large number of mediums and healers.

Cultural Background

I come from the catholic community in Goa, India. Goa was a Portuguese colony until 1961 and families like mine spoke Portuguese at home. I grew up on the music of the likes of Cliff and Elvis, Simon and Garfunkel and Leonard Cohen.

Although the study of eastern religions was to become the interest of my life, like any westerner studying eastern religions, I came at this from the outside.

In the 1960s, as part of Goa's integration into the mainstream of India, the study of Hindi was introduced as a compulsory subject in High School. My parents brought in tutors to teach me the script (devanagri script). Little was I to know that this study would prove highly relevant to me as later when I became interested in Hinduism and The Bhagavad-Gita, I was able to engage with the study of Sanskrit which used the same script. In fact many Indian Languages are offshoots of Sanskrit.

I do believe in past lives and feel so at home among the pantheon of Hindu Gods and Goddesses, that I have no doubt in my mind that a past life as a Hindu monastic is informing the deepest emotional drives in this present life.

My Journey

Ever since my early twenties, my search led me to read about as many teachers and teachings associated with eastern philosophy as came within my orbit. Travelers on the then hippie trail through Nepal and India had discovered Goa in the 1970s. Every week on the beaches there were flea markets where travelers from Europe sold their surplus possessions and books. It was through these books I bought that I was introduced to everything from the books of Carlos Castaneda, to the 'Perennial

Philosophy and I-Ching'. A different world opened before me. During this time it became clear that as a pupil of eastern philosophies, I would have to find a guru figure. When I came across the books related to the Russian mystic George Ivanovitch Gurdjieff, I felt I had come home.

As soon as I came to the UK, I made contact with teachers and groups associated with Gurdjieff, and this teaching became my focus for over 25 years.

In 2008, a chance meeting with the person and teachings of Ajahn Sumedho, the then abbot of Amravati, a Buddhist monastery north of London, opened my eyes to the Buddha- dharma (Buddhist teaching) and this has significantly informed my search from then on. It was through this connection that I encountered Ajahn Brahm on the Internet. The fact that for over two years now I have listened to an hour long talk of his mostly on You Tube, almost each and every day, probably qualifies me to call myself one of his many internet disciples.

About Section One: The Practice of Letting Go

In March 2013, the idea came into my head to try to summarise some of the essential teachings of Ajahn Brahm.

Ajahn Brahm is a world famous exponent of the Buddhist teaching. He is known for his storytelling (he is a really good raconteur), his jokes, and his ability to discuss the day-to-day problems and issues of life within the context of Buddhist ideas.

His You Tube talk called 'Four Ways of Letting Go' has some half a million hits since it was put out in 2010. This speaks for itself.

I started to listen to his talks and make little notes. I then divided the material into past, present and future. The reflections and insights are my own spin on what he has said. The idea is for a reader to get the gist, and if they wish to find out more, they can listen to his talks on the Internet. This is free. Both the reflections and insights 'came to me' without much effort on my part. I simply wrote down the words that popped into my head.

In this section, I have also written a bit on the Buddhist approach to dealing with difficult emotions, seeing a professional and resources on the net. There is also a section on happiness.

About Section Two: Buddhism, Hinduism, & Mystic Christianity

This consists of a series of personal reflections on the essence of Hinduism and Buddhism. Because I regard the Bhagavad-Gita as my personal bible, study of the Hindu scriptures has loomed large in my life. However in Buddhism as expounded by Ajahn Brahm and Ajahn Sumedho I have found exactly the same essential truth.

From my perspective the two traditions are simply sides of each other. They are also linked to the essential teaching of the Tao linking China, India and the Buddhist world as three sides of a triangle.

The Symbol On The Front Of The Book

In the symbolism of Hinduism the Universe is described in terms of 'Everything', 'Anything' and 'Infinity'. The Buddhists describe exactly the same truth with words such as 'Empty', Zero' and 'Nothing'. In the philosophy of the Tao, this same truth is described in the saying 'He who speaks does not know, He who knows does not speak.' Of course as any student of eastern philosophy is told ad infinitum is that these words are pointers only. They point to the ineffable indescribable experience of 'Cosmic Consciousness', to an experience of a dimension outside space and time yet including them also.

The symbol as drawn by me and rendered in an IT format by my collaborator Tim Lee attempts to combine the Ying-Yang figure representing duality (the Dwaita of Hinduism), with the Ba-Gua representing the Law of Change (Impermanence) in Buddhism and on either sides are Chinese characters representing the Tao.

The chapter on Gnostic Christianity was added as being a Christian by birth, and a student of the Gurdjieff teaching, this area has been relevant to me my whole life.

In the Hindu teaching, Christ, Buddha, Krishna and Muhammad are all 'Sons of God'. The deeper teachings are essentially the same. But these teachings have to be personally discovered. They cannot be verbalised.

SECTION ONE:
The Practice of Letting Go

Part 1: Letting Go Of The Past

My reflections on facing life's difficulties based on the You Tube talks of Ajahn Brahm.

1. Let go of doing hindsight

Particularly when bringing up painful memories of the past, the ordinary mind dreams up imaginary scenarios of how things might have been.

'If only I had done this…'

'Had I known what was round the corner...'

At several moments in our lives we have to make decisions, take the right or left fork of a road without knowing what lies ahead. The kinds of decisions we make generally will depend on our personality, our circumstances, our gut instinct, social factors etc.

The truth is that none of us can really predict how things will turn out. As the saying goes… 'Life is what happens when you're busy making other plans'.

There are no good or bad decisions. There are only the decisions we happen to have made.

Yet we can spend an amazing amount of useless time beating ourselves up over imaginary scenarios of what might have been, instead of concentrating on what we need to be doing right now.

As is well documented on the Internet, Ajahn Brahm found himself in a spot of bother, over the episode of full ordination of four Buddhist nuns in Australia. When interviewed he was asked the usual question 'With the aid of hindsight would you have done it again?' Ajahn answered very simply ...'I do not do hindsight'. Full stop.

Insight: Don't waste your energy doing hindsight. It is foolish to cry over spilt milk.

2. Let go of the idea of 'Why me?'

When something bad happens to us, we tend to ask the universe 'why me?'

If we look at the world around us, we can see that along with all the good stuff happening, there's also a lot of bad stuff. This is the nature of life on this planet.

It has always been this way.

If we look at the last 100 years there have been two world wars, and countless other disasters. Currently there are millions of refugees worldwide, who find themselves driven from their homes and surviving in the most squalid conditions.

If we look at the history of the world, the poor and disadvantaged have always had to eke out a living with very little control of their circumstances and fortunes.

It can sometimes seem that life is unfair, and bad things seem to happen to good people. The truth is that life is like that. Bad stuff is going to happen. It has to happen to someone.

Instead of reacting with 'why me?' can we perhaps have the courage to ponder 'why not me?'

Insight: Ask the universe 'why not me?'

3. Let go of seeking for revenge

People can sometimes hurt us; harm us, and say bad things about us big time.

It's easy to say 'let it go', but we know how hard, if not impossible it is for us to actually do this. We know that the desire for revenge is a form of anger that initially may give us a high, but it takes its toll and will run down our energy battery.

A less severe form of this is to bear someone a grudge.

It is essential for us to realise that we have to learn to forgive, not for the other person's sake but for ours. Carrying anger runs us down, impedes our growth, sullies our aura, and increases our chances of becoming mentally exhausted, stressed, anxious and depressed.

There is little doubt that latching onto some kind of religious belief can be very helpful. A Christian might remember the phrase 'Revenge is mine saieth The Lord'.

A Buddhist will be encouraged to take the view 'I should not retaliate. Karma will sort it out'. This issue is touched upon in the chapter on dealing with difficult emotions.

Insight: Carrying the desire for revenge blights us and drains our energies.

4. Let go of attachment to past suffering

It is said that on the spiritual path, a person will be quite happy about sacrificing their pleasures. Sacrificing their suffering is quite another matter.

Of the things a person is most loyal to it is to the memory of the bad things that have happened to them.

Consider this, say suppose you were given two sheets of paper and given these instructions: On paper one write down 10 good things that have happened to you in the last year, on paper two write down 10 bad things that have happened to you in the last year. Why is it that you will find paper two easy and paper one hard?

It is because painful memories are stored in a different email folder in our memory bank from our pleasures and blessings. We easily forget our blessings but seem to hold on to our painful memories like treasured possessions.

Eckhart Tolle, the world famous spiritual teacher has coined a term 'the pain body' which is described in his book 'The Power of Now'. This book is considered to be one of the most influential spiritual books of our generation and is purported to have transformed numerous lives, helping people understand how to escape painful prisons of the past and look at their lives with new eyes.

Insight: Inability to let go of past pain is one of the biggest drags on spiritual progress. It impedes our day-to-day life as well. Deeply understand what drains your energies and then ask: what can I do about it?

5. Let go of grief at the passing of a loved one

Have you ever considered the fact that when you cry for a loved one, you are actually crying for yourself?

Can you say that you are actually crying for the departed? Of course not.

In the Hindu scriptures they say that when a baby is born, the baby cries but the family around it smile and laugh. When a person dies the family cry, but it is said that the departed soul laughs. It laughs at having shaken off the body with all its earthly shackles and pains.

Ajahn Brahm says that grief, as it is encountered in the west is a cultural addition. It is not innate, but a culturally conditioned learned response. Ajahn says that for most of the nine years he lived as a Buddhist monk in Thailand, he lived in North East Thailand, which had neither been colonised nor influenced by the West. He encountered villages where he was the first white man they had ever seen. He describes his surprise at noticing that the population there did not grieve at deaths in the way people in the West did. They treated it in a much more matter of fact sort of way.

It is also interesting that there is now a vast literature on near death experiences, past and life regression therapy and also the work of spiritualist mediums such as Lisa Williams, James Van Praagh, Gordon Smith and Colin Fry, whose books are bestsellers. They all paint an interesting picture of what happens when we pass. It is something to think about.

Insight: The soul is eternal, the body is transient. Open to idea of celebrating the life and not mourning the death. In the Bhagavad-Gita, Krishna says 'The truly wise mourn neither for the living, nor for the dead'.

6. Let go of labels and personas

Can we see how distorting it is to reduce people and events to labels in our mind and in our speech?

Is a thief a thief or a person who has committed a theft?

Is a murderer a murderer or a person who has committed a murder?

Is a criminal a criminal or a person who has committed a crime?

Ajahn Brahm has spent substantial amounts of time teaching in prisons and helping prisoners.

He has approached them as good, whole persons who happen to have broken the law.

By treating them in this way, not just from the head but also from the heart, prisoners have found new self-esteem and have not reoffended. He says that one of the greatest complements he received was when he was specially called to an Australian prison in Perth and informed that none of the prisoners who he had taught had reoffended. This was singular in the prison service's experience.

In our own lives we can often slap on a label in relation to an adverse life event. Examples of this are things like 'grieving person', 'a victim', 'bankrupt' 'tragic case', 'loser', 'unemployed' and 'divorcee'. This kind of negative emotional overlay leads us to carry around a persona that only hinders us and does nothing for our self esteem.

Can we find a way to let it go?

Insight: Labels are like prison cells with the key on the inside. Understanding the prison cell of a limiting belief, allows one to open the door of the cell and walk out.

7. Let go of the idea that we learn from the failures of the past

By and large we do not, we learn much more by focusing on the successes of the past. The process of living is like a chicken farm. Ajahn Brahm frequently tells a farmyard-teaching story that his teacher Ajahn Chah frequently told. I didn't understand it at first. But after listening to the story a few times its significance dawned on me and it is utterly profound.

There were two chicken farmers, one stupid and one smart. The stupid chicken farmer would go into the henhouse every day to collect the produce. What do you think he collected? He collected the chicken shit and left the eggs to rot. What did he do with the chicken shit? He brought it into his house where it did no good. It only stank the place out. He brought no pleasure to his family and friends.

The smart chicken farmer, on the other hand, collected the shit but did not bring it into the house. He put it on the compost heap to create valuable fertiliser. What he brought into the house were the eggs from which he made an omelette to feed his family and took the rest of the eggs to the market to sell for cash.

The process of living is like a chicken farm. It produces both eggs and shit. The two are inseparable. The choice people have is to resemble the stupid chicken farmer or to attempt to emulate the smart chicken farmer.

Which kind of chicken farmer are you?

Note: I have used the word 'shit', instead of detritus, dung, and excreta, as Ajahn Brahm is very insistent on using this word in all his public talks. He insists the Buddha advocated that his monks used 'real living language' to get the message across and should not exhibit false modesty.

Insight: The process of living is continually experimental. We make mistakes and we have our successes. The idea that we can avoid making mistakes is nonsense. As a learning experience, focus on your successes (the chicken eggs in the story) and leave the failures and mistakes (the chicken shit in the story) behind. You grow by focusing on the successes of the past not raking up the failures and mistakes. Learn to let mistakes and failures of the past go.

Part 2: Letting Go In The Present

8. Let go of allowing other people to control our personal happiness

Preoccupation with what other people think of us, whether they have a good opinion of us, whether they like us and so forth, is one of the greatest inner slaveries and negative burdens that we can carry around in our minds.

Are you worried about how you are perceived?

Are you worried about whether you 'fit in'?

Do you know your 'place in society'?

Ajahn Brahm often recounts the saying 'When you are 20 you are finding your place in the world, you wear particular clothes, designer labels and so on. You worry what people think.

When you are 40, you are self-confident and dress the way you want. You couldn't care less what people think. When you are 60 you realise nobody was ever thinking about you anyway!

Why? Because they have been busy thinking about their own stuff. Do you think they have ever had time or interest to think about you?

Live for yourself. Do not live for others (as alluded to above).

Do not be a mental slave to non-existent masters.

Insight: If you want to feel free, you have to find a way to be happy with the person you are. Live in your own skin and be free from worrying 'what other people think'.

9. Let go of doing more than one thing at a time

In life we have to play many roles (father, mother, spouse, provider, home maker, friend, office worker, business associate, mate down at the pub…).

We carry far too many things in our head, which can wear us down and stress us out.

If we wish to keep our sanity and be effective in what we do in life we need to focus on two things:

The first thing is to simplify our life and deal with the priorities. This is the equivalent of sorting out your computer. Delete those files that are no longer needed. Archive those files and folders, which you need to store, and you do not need in your face. Set up a system where junk mail and spam are not allowed past your firewall. Delete all emails you don't recognise. This will leave you the mental space to see and deal with only the data you need to see and want to see.

The second thing is to give the situation or person in front of you your undivided attention. Only carry the concern for what you should be doing right now, right here.

One of Ajahn Brahm's often-repeated teaching stories is taken from one of Tolstoy's short stories.

In this story, an emperor obsessed with finding the secret of life worked out that everything boils down to only three questions. When is the right time? Who is the right person? What is the right thing to do? The answer?

They are as follows. The right time is right now. The right person is the person you are with. The right thing to do is to care. Right now when you are with someone else your duty is to care for them. Focus on what they need.

Much of our day we are with ourselves. We should devote this time caring for ourselves, seeing what we need.

Give yourself 'me time'.

Learn to relax.

Insight: If you wish to be effective learn to focus only on the task at hand. Learn to live in the here and now. Learn to regard the past as history, and the future as a mystery and the present as a gift. What you are doing right here and right now will determine and inform the future.

10. Let go of the idea that you have to 'improve yourself'

Having spent 25 years sitting among various spiritual seekers within the context of meditation type groups (non Buddhist) in London, it has amazed me, that even after years of being told that the aim was to 'see oneself as one was warts and all' there were devoted students who continued to hold onto the idea that they were there to 'improve themselves', become 'better people' as it were, more competent and successful in their day to day lives. Whereas there were some who easily cottoned onto the difference between witnessing oneself as one was without criticism, there were others who were simply unable to take on the idea of seeing oneself without criticism.

As human beings we are by our very nature limited and imperfect in many ways.

The aim of the spiritual path that these writings allude to is to find that place and perspective within ourselves, from whence we can see ourselves without criticism, love ourselves warts and all, accept our limitations and mistakes with humour,

And learn to laugh at ourselves and learn to laugh at life.

They say that charity begins at home. If we can be truly charitable towards ourselves does it not follow that we can be charitable to others? Everyone is tarred with the same brush of humanity; all are in the same boat. For me the words of Jesus 'love thy neighbour as thyself' means just this kind of acceptance of 'things as they are' what Buddhists call 'the Dharma'

Insight: This is how you are right here, right now. Improve your acceptance of how you are warts and all. You are perfect as you are.

11. Let go of the 'fault-finding mind'

Falling slave to a strong fault-finding mental attitude is one of the chief causes of negative emotion that enhances the likelihood of becoming chronically angry, depressed, stressed and burnt out. No fun at all. All of us know such persons. Are they fun to be with?

This tendency takes the form of constantly looking for things that are 'wrong with the world.' 'The world is not good enough' or 'people are not good enough.' This can also take the form of self-criticism such as 'I am not good enough'.

I was profoundly moved when, reading through Ajahn Sumedho's book 'The Mind and The Way', he describes the correct understanding of 'Metta'. As anyone who studies Buddhism even at the most basic level will know

'Metta or loving-kindness' is a central concept. I quote from the book….page 40 'Metta does not necessarily mean liking anything at all. It means an attitude of not dwelling on the unpleasantness or faults of any situation inside or outside oneself.'

So Metta can be seen as the opposite of the fault-finding mind, as a practical antidote to it.

Correctly understood and applied, perhaps we can open to the perspective that: 'The world is good enough, people are good enough and most importantly that 'I am good enough.'

Insight: We are limited, imperfect beings and will always be so. Can we open to the idea of focusing on the 'good' in others and ourselves and the good in the world around us rather than focusing on the negative? Focus on your positive aspects.

12. Let go of giving, expecting something in return

In our workplaces, in our social circle, among our relatives and friends, we can always find some people that seem to approach situations with the attitude 'what's in it for me?'. And then there are others who seem to exude the sense of 'how can I help?'

Which kind of person do you gravitate to? If you needed something done, if you had a job contract to hand out which kind of person would you employ or enlist?

The Buddha and Jesus both taught that we needed to learn to give. To give expecting nothing in return. Because that was the most sacred way, the most enlightened way to live a life.

When we give the very best of ourselves to our partner, our family, our workplace, our society, we create the best possible conditions for both others and ourselves.

Is this what Jesus meant in the saying ' In giving you receive'?

When we give in order to get something back, not only do we not know what we will get back, but we set up a negative psychological cycle, where we are constantly preoccupied with our conceptions of what specific persons and the wider world owe us. This is what, the 'what's in it for me' mentality engenders.

Whether you are a Christian or Muslim, with a belief in some form of judgement at death or a Buddhist or Hindu with the concept of a 'karma' which you take from life to life, or an agnostic, which kind of life mentality would you consider most valuable?

My observation has been that for those folks who give of themselves selflessly 'The Lord does indeed provide'. If you give to the universe the universe gives to you.

Insight: Can we open to the idea that it is in giving that we receive and it is in self-centeredness that we create the perfect recipe for personal misery? Understand that when you give expecting nothing in return you are creating a positive energy in yourself.

13. Let go of thinking about life, instead of living it

When we eat at a restaurant we read the menu. The menu is not a substitute for the actual meal. Ultimately we can only know the taste of the food by actually eating it. This direct taste of the meal is personal to each one of us, and it is final so far as the meal is concerned. The menu is at best a guide and pointer, no more.

Our actual experience of our life, the actual taste of it is like the eating of a meal.

What we think about life is the menu. We carry around all kinds of ideas and opinions about who our friends are, who our enemies are, what life is about and so on and so forth. This is all like a restaurant menu. Is it wise to confuse this for the taste of the meal?

Ajahn Brahm tells a teaching story about the Chinese sage Lao Tzu. In the story, Lao Tzu would allow a student to accompany him on his evening walk on condition that complete silence would be maintained. Coming to a ridge in the mountain, a student forgot the rule and blurted out 'what a beautiful sunset!'. Lao Tzu turned back in reprimand. When his other students asked what had gone so wrong, the great master gave this most profound piece of wisdom, 'When that student uttered 'what a beautiful sunset', he was not watching the sunset. He was only watching his words'.

This particular story is worth pondering over and over.

We can live in our thoughts, live in our inner chatter. We chatter to ourselves incessantly and this prevents us from seeing and experiencing the proverbial sunset that is right in front of us. We spend our time talking to ourselves about it.

Sometimes we cannot taste the food right in front of us on our plate because we are too caught up in the menu.

Insight: Open to tasting the actual experience of life in the here and now. Live in experience, not in thought. Thinking and philosophising about life gives us the experience of thought and thinking, not the taste of life and living.

14. Let go of the idea that you need to go so fast

Ajahn Brahm tells the story of how one spring morning in Perth, instead of being driven up the road to his monastery, he decided to walk. He describes his amazement at being able to take in the sights and sounds of the natural world in a way he never could, while speeding by in a car.

This is the difference between going for a ramble in the countryside as opposed to driving by in a car.

Life can be like that. In our fast-paced life we try and cram in too many things in our day. So many things, in fact, that we allow ourselves physically and psychologically no time at all, to simply stand and stare.

The beauty of life, the beauty of the present moment is something we can so easily ignore in the blind activity that we call 'being busy'.

Insight: If we wish to enjoy the beauty that is all around us, we need to slow down and open to cultivating stillness.

15. Let go of the idea that we need to 'get things right'

Is there such a thing as right and wrong (in an ordinary sense, not a criminal sense)?

We always seem to obsess about getting things right, not 'getting things wrong'.

As we look into this we see that we can only act in keeping with our previous experience, our personality, our upbringing, our social class and cultural setting etc.

Two persons from different cultural and educational milieus will react to one and the same type of event in two different ways, and in both cases it would be right for them.

Take the example of females growing up in orthodox Middle Eastern cultures versus growing up in Europe or North America. We can see that 'getting things right' can mean very different things to these two groups.

As we begin to see that what we do is very dependant on whom we are, we begin to find acceptance and tolerance to both others and ourselves. We begin to see that there is no black and white, only various shades of grey.

Insight: As we understand and appreciate our personal subjectivity, in practically everything, we open to the idea of not seeing the world and events around us in terms of right and wrong, black and white. We stop obsessing about 'getting things right'. This makes us much less stressed. Do the best you can and leave it as that.

5. Let go of the idea that life should be fair

Some folk are born with so many advantages, such as being able to grow up in prosperous and loving families. All the conditions are provided for them to make the best of themselves to reach their potential.

Some folk are born with so many disadvantages. They grow up with too many brothers and sisters often in conditions of deprivation and neglect. Adversity blights their potential. You get the picture? Where is the fairness in this? But this is how it is on the earth plane. And it is not fair.

In my own life I have noticed that when I have suffered and complained to myself about life being unfair, it has arisen because in my limited emotional perspective I have compared myself to persons real and imagined who are better off or more successful than me. When the heart can open to the real or even imagined plight of persons less fortunate than myself, suffering vanishes.

On the ladder of life can we not only look up at the person above us on the ladder, but also look down at the person below us?

Insight: As we emotionally open to the plight of those who are less fortunate than us, we become more emotionally accepting of our lot. We start to let go of the idea that life should be fairer to us than other people. Develop gratitude for what you have.

17. Let go of the idea that you have to criticise yourself

The drive to constantly 'improve' is deeply etched in our psyche. I suspect that the roots are deeply bound in the whole development of western civilisation. This includes other cultures that follow the western model. From kindergarten we are consciously and unconsciously encouraged to compete, do well at school, get to the top of the class for example. This leads to a mentality of winners and losers. It contributes to self-criticism, which some folk actually see as a virtue.

Having sat in spiritual circles for some 25 years where participants are encouraged to bare their souls, in what passes for a safe environment, I have frequently heard the expression 'I hate myself'. This has often come from individuals who others would consider as 'regular guys', reasonably successful, who have made their way in the world, married with normal families, own property for example, and yet they 'hate themselves'. Amazing.

It is said that when the Dalai Lama visited the US in the 1970's and was doing a tour of college campuses, young men and women used the expression 'I hate myself', 'self-loathing'. At this time the Dalai Lama was using translators who had difficulty in making sense of this, as there was no equivalent in Tibetan. I suspect that this is because this emotion is a particular product of western civilisation. It is probably absent in indigenous cultures not tainted by the west.

Growing up in a devout catholic family, I was fed on the idea of sin and punishment, of the need to work at redemption. So western religions contribute to the feeling that 'I am imperfect'.

On the spiritual path alluded to in these writings we are encouraged to see our self-criticism not as a virtue but as a vice.

In the chapter on Difficult Emotions I discuss the 'I hate myself' feeling some more.

Insight: Open to the idea that you are fine as you are. Learn to love yourself as you are. You may not be a saint, but you are certainly not a sinner.

18. Let go of focusing on the weeds in your garden

Ajahn Brahm, in his talks, has sometimes compared life to a garden. Gardens have things we like, the flowers for instance, and also things we tend to dislike such as 'the weeds'.

As we develop insight into the nature of life and the laws of nature we begin to see that the weeds in our garden have a legitimate right to exist.

Can we learn to accept them, perhaps even love them?

The weeds are the various 'imperfections' we see in our self, our various 'faults', perhaps things we are not terribly proud of, things we don't boast about.

Yet these are part of us and always will be. Can we be more accepting of ourselves, as we are, and not focus on sweeping things under the carpet?

Perhaps the way to approach this wisely is not to focus on removing the weeds but instead to learn to water the flowers without watering the weeds. Flowers will then have a chance to flood the garden and the weeds will tend to die back.

Insight: Can we focus on the many good qualities we have? What we focus on will grow. Focus on the flowers and nice plants in your garden. Leave the slugs, snails and weeds to do their own thing. They also have a right to exist. Love your garden as it is.

19. Let go of suffering over events you have no choice over.

There are some parts of our life we have reasonable control over. We can reasonably be expected to keep on the right side of the law for instance.

There are bits of our lives we have only partial control over. Our health, family situations and situations at work are some of these. Even if you live healthily it does not guarantee a long, disease free life. However 'good' you are, you do not control the actions of others among your family and friends, whose actions may impact on you.

As for your workplace, most folk do not control their boss, their work colleagues or how their company will perform against their competitors or on the stock exchange.

We have no control over large chunks of our life.

Accidents, illnesses, storms, earthquakes and tsunamis, both real and proverbial can strike us without warning. Our business could go bust, our spouse can run off with our best friend, we could be struck down by a speeding police car…the list can go on and on.

Life is inherently unstable and uncertain. As we begin to emotionally understand this fact, we realise that we don't have to take things personally. This reduces suffering.

You do not have a choice over the hand of cards life deals out to you.

What you do have an amazing amount of control over is how you emotionally adapt to the situation.

Insight: Remember to define a problem as something that has a solution, as something you can do something about. If a situation has no solution or is out of our control, then it is not a problem. Don't waste time and energy on it. Instead put this time and energy into learning to live with the situation and adapt to it.

20. Let go of taking things too personally.

A spouse or close family member may make a caustic remark to us. In our workplace a similar scenario may play itself out. We are prone to take this as a personal affront.

We can carry this kind of thing in our heads and it can drive us nuts.

Do we consider enough that the event may have nothing or very little to do with us?

Folk make caustic comments and insult others for a variety of reasons. Very often they are having an 'off day', they may have social and medical problems in their life, which stress them out and impact on their behaviour.

By taking things personally, we live on the level of a soap opera, where nobody's happy, and everyone is bitching about everyone else.

Do you want to be part of this film set?

Insight: Taking life too personally is one of the most terrible forms of inner slavery. Do the right thing by other people, but don't stress about what they think about you. Be free of this kind of worry. You will find this is very liberating.

21. Let go of asking the world what it can never give you.

Ajahn Brahm recounts how he encountered a businessman in a hurry, who asked him: This thing 'Dukka', in Buddhism, what is it? The answer that came out of his mouth surprised even Ajahn.

Ajahn said: 'Dukka is asking of the world what it can never give you'.

This is now a recurring phrase in Ajahn Brahm's talks, which is so apt.

So what are the things we ask?

Do we ask of our boss at work what they cannot give us?

Do we ask of our spouse what they can never give us?

Do we ask of our world (our personal social environment) what it can never give us?

And most importantly, do we ask of ourselves, that which is beyond our capacity to give? What is not in our gift?

Looking at life through rose tinted glasses and carrying around unrealistic expectations, is one of the chief reasons we set ourselves up to be disappointed.

Insight: If we can avoid carrying unrealistic expectations of what the world can give us, we are bound to live much happier lives, much less likely to get divorced and be much better and fun companions to our family, friends and work colleagues.

22. Let go of the prisons of your life

A prison is anyplace you don't want to be. If you are in a job that you don't like then your office is a prison. If you are in a marriage or relationship that you don't like then this situation is your prison. If you're sick in bed with an illness and you hate it then your body is a prison. Anyplace you don't want to be is a prison.

Have you come across persons that never seem to be happy with the job they have and are frequently changing jobs? Have you come across persons that are never happy with the partner they have? Have you come across persons that are ill and cannot take it?

Of course we have, and to varying extents the above may apply to us.

The 'solution' is not to change your job, change your partner or even get better from your illness. Instead one needs to find a new relationship with the things that give us hassle. A change of attitude.

A change of attitude is possibly the most powerful energy in the spiritual toolkit.

It can transform our lives.

There is no such thing as the perfect job, the perfect partner or perfect health.

If things seem perfect right now, enjoy it-while it lasts. If we expect the good times to last forever we are labouring under an illusion.

We need to cultivate an attitude of 'making peace' with whatever situation we are in.

Insight: Freedom does not come from pleasant circumstances. It comes from an understanding of the nature of life and being able to make peace with the circumstances one finds oneself in. Freedom is a matter of attitude not circumstance.

23. Let go of conceit

In normal language conceit tends to refer to a feeling of superiority over other people.

In the Buddhist lexicon this word refers to three kinds of situations:

1) Feeling one is better than others
2) Feeling one is worse than others
3) Feeling one is the same as others.

Isn't this interesting!

We consciously or unconsciously compare ourselves to other people. Whether we have more intelligence, money or beauty than them. This can lead to so much unnecessary angst. Can we open to the idea that we are all unique? Like apples and pears are both unique. Neither fruit is better than the other. Can we make peace with the unique person we are?

Insight: Don't compare yourself to others. You are who you are. Learn to live with yourself, love yourself and be confident in your own skin.

24. Let go of the idea that you need more

In our materialistic society we are constantly being brainwashed with the idea that we need more and more. Our industrial society survives on folk buying more and more things. With the availability of easy credit, we see folk flooding to the shopping malls, which to some extent resemble a new religion, buying things they don't really need with money they don't really have. All of us know folk who are addicted to retail therapy and maxed out on their credit cards.

In truth, if we are not hungry, cold, homeless or ill, everything else is in our heads. Will getting more 'stuff' make us happier? Can we see that hankering after more 'stuff', interferes with ones' enjoyment of the stuff one already has. Can we perhaps focus more on learning to enjoy the stuff we currently have? Aspiring to want what you already have?

Insight: Understand that when you want more, you are interfering with your ability to enjoy what you already have. Learn to be content with things as they are right now.

25. Let go of the idea that you will do something about a 'problem' at a future time

As we become more and more clear that the future is uncertain and unpredictable, it becomes clearer that we cannot put off things till the proverbial tomorrow.

This does not mean that we need do more than we need to do today. It means that tomorrow can be well and truly another day.

Every day we are making ourselves what we are. Ajahn Brahm repeatedly says that ones future success, ones future happiness is being constructed right now, right here.

Is it wise to get stuck in the future?

Is it wise to get stuck in the past?

Or is it the smart thing to get stuck in what's needed right now.

Sometimes there's nothing one can do.

The smart thing then is to do nothing-right now.

Insight: Put your energy into what's needed right now. If there's nothing to do then put your energy into relaxation and doing nothing.

26. Let go of impatience

Because we do not control things, in the way we sometimes imagine and we have to endure circumstances, for indefinite periods of time, it becomes clear that we need to understand patience. We need to learn to be patient. But we can only be patient for one moment at a time. Yesterday is gone. We cannot be patient tomorrow. We can only be patient today.

Insight: Learning the art of patience is to learn one of life's great virtues. The practice of mindfulness helps us take one moment at a time. We have to learn to embrace the emotion of impatience, accept it and work with it.

27. Let go of personal criticism about 'stuffing up'

Life is difficult. We cannot avoid making mistakes. Can we learn to accept this as part of the course, as part of life? Can we also see that when we are not too worried about making mistakes, we actually make fewer mistakes?

Ajahn Brahm often refers to the 70% rule in his talks. We don't need to get things 100% right. 70% is fine. This is realistic and achievable.

Insight: Pitch your expectations at 7/10 rather than 10/10 when focusing on expectations we have of ourselves, the people in our lives and the world in general. Such a benchmark reduces your stress. It is foolish to walk around with unrealistic goals. It will make you a much happier person.

28. Let go of the tendency to take criticism to heart

When we are criticised, our reaction is instant.

When we are praised, we have no instant reaction.

As we understand how our 'ego' operates, it is easier to see how we react to criticism.

When someone else is criticised, no matter how unfairly, it hardly hits us in the stomach. After all it's not our ego that's involved.

Each of us has an ego that is easily hurt. However if one forgives oneself for having a petty ego, this helps us to not take criticism too seriously. Then it's much easier to let things go and not bear a grudge.

Insight: As we learn to understand and accept our petty ego for what it is, it becomes harder for us to take criticism by others too personally. This is a big freedom.

29. Let go of trying to be a control freak

We tend to be under the illusion that if we do not control things, our life will go wrong. As we begin to see that we in fact do not control outer events, we begin to see that nothing can go wrong, because we do not control things in the first place.

In outer life the blind wish to exert control, leads to anxiety and stress.

Ajahn Brahm in his talks on meditation is at pains to point out, that an effort to control the mind, to force it, leads nowhere.

Peace in life as in meditation comes from the wisdom of 'going with the flow'.

Insight: Understand that trying to control what is not in your power to control is like labouring under the illusion that you can control the weather. Use your energy to go with the flow and adapt to circumstances as they arise.

30. Let go of the 'what's in it for me' attitude

All life is interdependent. Everything depends upon everything else.

No human being is truly independent. We know that when we are very young, very old or very sick our survival depends upon others. Similarly man is dependant on nature to provide him with his sustenance. Families, work teams, and social groups are also systems where groups of individuals are interdependent.

An attitude of 'how can I help?' is in keeping with the ethos that allows successful group functioning. An attitude of 'what's in it for me?' does the opposite.

Insight: Understand that egocentric attitudes will get you nowhere. You cannot exist and survive as an independent entity. Seek to understand instead the laws of interdependence.

31. Let go of wasting time on insoluble problems

Ajahn Brahm describes a problem as something that has a solution. If there is no solution, it is not a problem. Much of life can be uselessly fretted away pondering insoluble issues particularly from the past and fearful scenarios projected into the future.

Insight: Remember the words of the Serenity Prayer which goes as follows: 'God, give me the serenity to accept the things I cannot change, the courage to change the things I can, and wisdom to know the difference.' *Reinhold Niebuhr*

32. Let go of indecision

Sometimes we can be caught up in the notion that we cannot make a decision or decide on a course of action. It is helpful to realise that there are no good or bad decisions.

Things are not black and white. Things are a shade of grey and can even be mottled and speckled. One can only make the best decision one can at the time, and we need to let go of doing hindsight.

Ajahn Brahm says in his talks that we should first get as much relevant information as possible.

Our decision should not come from stupidity, not from fear, not from selfish personal desire and not from anger or ill will.

Ideally our decisions should be practical, skilful, cause no harm to others and be of benefit to a wider world and to oneself.

Insight: Whatever decision you make is fine. The important thing is whether you are 'coming from the right place'.

33. Let go of anger

We can carry around a lot of anger, both towards other people, the world in general and also towards ourselves.

One of the reasons we get angry is because we are tired. We carry so much stuff in our minds that we get exhausted. And when we are angry, we drain our energy battery and this worsens the tiredness. A vicious circle.

The antidote to anger is to cultivate forgiveness. Although this forgiveness is directed to persons and events outside, the actual focus of healing is our inside. By forgiving we help ourselves. By failing to do so we hurt ourselves.

Insight: Carrying anger is like carrying a leaking bucket. This bucket holds our life energy. We hurt ourselves if we cannot find a way to stem the leak. Find a way to diffuse your anger.

34. Let go of the idea that 'I can get what I want if I try hard enough'

People can sometimes 'kill themselves' trying to achieve various goals, only to find that they either can't do it or that the goal did not live up to its expectation, and did not give them the happiness and satisfaction they were hoping for.

The development of 'will power' is not necessarily a good thing. It can lead to growth of the personal ego and to a sense of personal power both of which can actively make people unhappy.

Perhaps what one needs to search for is what Ajahn Brahm calls "wisdom power".

Insight: The cultivation of 'will power' is not what it is cracked up to be. It can even be an enemy to you and your happiness. Seek to cultivate "wisdom power" instead.

35. Let go of the idea that 'life is hard'

When we say that 'life is hard' we drag in emotional scenarios from the past and the projections of similar scenarios in the future.

Life lived, a moment at a time, an hour at a time, a day at a time, is not hard.

Is going to work on a Monday morning hard? It is only hard if you emotionally project, on what a Monday morning means to you. Living life is the easy part. Thinking about life is the difficult bit.

Insight: Life lived in the moment and by the day is not hard. It simply is as it is. Life is hard when we live in our thoughts instead of living inside our factual experience.

36. Let go of the idea that 'the grass is greener on the other side'

The ordinary mind is unable to see things in perspective. When envying one person's money luck for example, the same envying mind will ignore problems that the individual may have in other departments, such as their relationship and family or their health. For the envying mind, it is quite possible to envy one person's wealth, another person's marriage, a third person's children and a fourth person's seemingly robust health. It is quite common for people to envy Hollywood celebrities for their fame and fortune. Do people realise that stable marriages and happy families are the exception and not the rule in Hollywood? Would you truly want this for yourself?

Insight: The nature of the envying mind is generally grounded in fantasy. This type of mind is devoid of holistic perspective. Don't fall prey to it. Find the positives in your own life.

37. Letting go in meditation

Deeply peaceful states are experienced in meditation when we allow our selves to 'fall into' the 'witness state'. This has to be experienced to be known. However it is about the experience of allowing the free flow of thoughts and feelings to occur without getting caught up in them.

In ordinary life we are conditioned to do things and get things done. In meditation practice we endeavour to explore exactly the reverse. We 'try' to open to the experience of doing nothing and getting nothing done, simply opening to the experience of 'being without doing'. This calls for a deep relaxation and a 'letting go' of strivings, goals and aims.

Ajahn Brahm's talks associated with his meditation retreats cover all aspects of this area of practice. An example of this is the talk called 'being no-one going nowhere'

This was an introductory talk to attendees at his 10-day retreat in April 2012. Listen to it.

Part 3: Letting Go Of The Future

38. Let go of the idea that 'I will be happy in the future'

This is one of the primary delusions of the thinking mind. There is no happiness in the future. We do not know the future, and consequently we cannot say whether circumstances for happiness or unhappiness will be our lot.

We often think: 'When I get this, or when that happens then I shall be all right, then I shall be happy'. Things don't work that way. Wanting generates craving. Craving is notoriously unfaithful as once you get something you want, after a brief honeymoon, you will want something else. There is no end to it.

We can only be happy right here, right now. Not in the future.

Insight: You can only be happy in the here and now. Who knows what tomorrow will bring. Live one day at a time.

39. Let go of trying to get anywhere

The future is unknown. How can we try to get anywhere?

It is interesting that we make up our life story in arrears.

Life is what happens to us when we are busy making other plans.

A Woody Allen quote that is utterly profound goes as follows:

Q: How do you make God laugh?

A: Tell him your future plans.

Life happens to us as it happens to happen. Because our ego needs to feel that it has power, it tells us the story of our lives in such a way that it seeks to convince us that we are in control of events. After all, who wants to feel powerless?

As we begin to see this we can perhaps open to the present moment without trying to control.

Insight: There is nowhere to go except into the moment. Live in the moment.

40. Let go of making long-term plans

Life is uncertain. Hence plans and promises can only be tentative.

How can cast iron guarantees be given?

Of course they can be given. But can they be worth the paper they're written on?

Insight: Don't waste your time and energy making cast iron long term plans. Keep plans tentative. Design your plans around constant adaptation to ever changing circumstances.

41. Let go of unrealistic expectations

Ajahn Brahm's definition of 'Dukka' is 'asking of the world what it can never give you'.

We need to become more accepting of limitations and shortcomings, both in ourselves and in those around us. Thus our expectations become more grounded in reality, and we can enjoy happier, more peaceful, more satisfying and less stressed lives.

Insight: Let your expectations be governed by wisdom. Keep your outer goals realistic. Cultivate equanimity and peace of mind.

Part 4: Dealing With Difficult Emotions

42. Depression

Life can be depressing. Let's face it. We do our best. We struggle so hard. And things don't work out. We get stressed out and depleted. We try to feel good about life, about people and about the world. But it doesn't work out. Things get us down.

What to do?

Make peace with your feelings of depression. Don't try to fight them. Open to embracing depression with love and acceptance. Open to the knowledge that nothing lasts forever. All things must pass. The feelings of depression will run their course and pass. We simply need to be patient.

Insight: If we can accept depressive episodes as part and parcel of our lives, and learn to live with these feelings instead of fighting them, we actually get better quicker.

43. Anxiety

Anxiety can be part of life. We can become anxious about a whole load of things.

Some of the things we fear are real and some are imagined. When you're going through it, the difference doesn't matter, does it? Can we embrace our anxiety?

Accept it as part of who we are? Make peace with it? We may not like feeling anxious, but life is like that. Not all bits are nice.

Insight: Anxiety and anxious periods can be part of life. Accept and make peace with it. By having patience things get better.

44. Stress

Life will invariably contain varying levels of stress. If everything goes hunky dory we can expect to have a stress free life. When things don't go according to plan, assuming that we have a plan, life becomes stressful.

As we open to the fact that there will be times when things are hunky dory and other times where things don't go according to plan, we open to the fact that stress is part and parcel of life.

Can we accept it? Can we make peace with it?

Insight: On the one hand we have to accept stress. However a lot of our stress comes from trying to control aspects of our lives that we cannot in fact control. By learning to go with the flow rather than fighting the current our stress levels drop.

45. Anger

There can be a lot to be angry about. When our rights are violated, for instance. When something we deem as ours is taken from us. When we are hurt and harmed. The list can go on and on.

Whereas it may feel perfectly legitimate to feel anger, we also need to feel, see and understand what it does to us. It drains our energy and poisons our psyche.

What to do? We have to acknowledge our anger, and make peace with the fact that we carry anger. However, part of this making peace process is to search for a way to draw out its poison. The teaching on metta and forgiveness can help with this. It will also definitely help to seek the help of a priest, a Buddhist monk, or a similar type of counselor or helpful person. But we have to take the first step. Perhaps we will come to understand that 'forgiving those who trespass against us' as the Lord's Prayer goes, is more about helping ourselves rather than helping someone else.

Insight: Anger drains you; find a way of letting it go. Meditation helps.

46. Fear

'Fear, is finding fault with the future.'

The more we contemplate this saying of Ajahn Brahm, the more we can understand why we feel fearful. However, the truth is that we simply do not know what the future holds, and hence our fears are unfounded.

But we continue to feel fear, don't we?

Can we accept the fact that as human beings we will by our very nature be prone to feeling all kind of fears? Can we make peace with this aspect of how we are?

Actually almost all fear in human life fits into two categories. We fear that what we have or think we have will be lost or taken from us. Or we fear that we will not get what we want, or that things and events will not shape up the way we want.

The Buddhist approach to dealing with fear is to deeply understand it. From this understanding a quality of stoicism develops. The energy of fear is transformed into the energy of acceptance and adaptation.

In this context there is a famous Zen saying; 'The Way is easy for one who can live without preferences'. The cultivation of 'Fearlessness' is a central concern in practical Buddhism.

Insight: Learning to live in the here and the now and cultivating mindfulness is the best antidote to fear.

47. Sadness

Is there such a thing as a life without sadness?

If you can experience joy then you will also experience sadness.

When we are sad we have to accept this as part of life. We have to make peace with it. But we do not have to wallow in sadness. Let it pass on.

Insight: Don't wallow in sadness. Accept it when it comes and let it go.

48. Disgust

From time to time we will feel disgusted at something or other.

Sometimes this comes from a sense of false modesty and false morality.

For instance, persons who are proud of their 'high moral standards' can look down 'with disgust' on others who they do not regard as their moral equals.

It can be interesting to see where disgust comes from.

Yet this is part of our nature. Can we make peace with it whilst trying to see where it comes from?

Insight: Try not to be dominated by disgust. This can often arise from an unhealthy preoccupation with the lives of others. Let this go.

49. Hatred

When we love something, we hate its opposite. If you love the light you will hate the darkness. If you love 'good', you will hate 'evil'. If you love 'God', you will hate 'The Devil'. Yet can the light exist without the dark? The concept of good only exists against the concept of evil. Can you have a good god without a bad devil?

As human beings we live in a world of duality. Fame and infamy, honour and dishonour, health and illness, good fortune and bad fortune, good and evil, are the sky we live under. Like the days and the seasons, sometimes it is cloudy, sometimes sunny, sometimes hot, sometimes cold, sometimes floods, sometimes droughts and of course, sometimes nice normal, pleasant weather.

As we understand our world both inner and outer, both love and hate can appear differently. When we hate another person, can we at least try to put ourselves in their shoes, and see the world through their eyes?

Insight: Hate is only the other side of conditional love. As one explores the cultivation of unconditional love, hate and hatred start to weaken and disappear.

50. Jealousy and envy

As we begin to accept that life is not fair, we begin to accept the fact that others will be lucky in ways that we are unlucky, that others will have more than us, others that seem to have it all.

This may be true in part, but we can also project all sorts of fantasies on others.

Jealousy can sometimes be very poisonous to one that feels it. Like anger.

If we notice we are jealous, we need to first acknowledge it as part of the human condition. We need to forgive ourselves for feeling jealous. If we are able to look into it further we may find that we have a disordered perspective. Perhaps jealousy falls away when we are able to live in the moment and be more accepting of our lot in life.

Insight: Jealousy and envy are based on the false premise on what we believe other people have. Find gratitude in your own life.

51. Guilt

Buddhism is a path that does not do guilt. It is not encouraged.

Life is not perfect. People are not perfect. Mistakes will happen.

The ancient word associated with repentance in early Christianity is 'metanoia'.

This is a Greek word that means 'to change'.

When we discover that we have done something that we are not happy with, we have to learn to forgive ourselves. We seek to change. We should not expend energy beating ourselves up. We have to let go of guilt. There are many references of how to do this in Ajahn Brahm's talks.

Insight: Guilt often arises from the need to be perfect. By accepting yourself as you are, guilt will disappear.

52. Boredom

When we are feeling bored what do we do? We switch on the TV, pick up the paper, open the fridge, make ourselves a drink, find a snack, or find something else to do.

As we explore the nature of boredom we see that it is just another emotion. Not dramatic as anger or 'love'. It's…boring.

The trick is to acknowledge it, accept it and wait. It will pass.

Insight: Be patient with boredom. It will pass.

53. Low self esteem

Part of the reason we can have so called 'low self esteem' is that consciously or unconsciously we are comparing ourselves to others. Also we are taking on the spoken or unspoken opinions of others. It is surprising how much of our human interpersonal communication is non-verbal.

If persons who feel they are afflicted with this self-labeling can become more self aware, they can put themselves under the influence of people and books that can genuinely help them improve their confidence.

Insight: As we learn to love ourselves as we are and accept ourselves as we are, we learn to cultivate high self-esteem.

54. Worry too much

Some of us are terrible worriers. It's our nature.

To some extent if we analyse the nature of our worries, we find that they are without much foundation. We know that worry doesn't solve anything and yet we worry, don't we? Perhaps we have to learn to accept our worrying nature as part of the type of person we are. It's not very pleasant, but that's us. We need to make peace with our worrying.

Insight: When we worry less about the fact that we are worrying too much, we actually worry less.

Part 5: Notebook Reflections On Happiness

Happiness is not a destination. It is a mode of travelling.

As we understand what happiness is, we see that craving is an obstacle to happiness.

It is said that when a person experiences nirvana, they no longer obsess about ordinary happiness. This leads to a deep peace that is experienced as a deep state of happiness.

It is said that this peace and this happiness is not dependant on the satisfaction of craving, and is actually dependant on the falling away of craving. In this state one is okay with what is. Let go of the idea that a persistent state of happiness is an attainable objective.

Ajahn Brahm says that when he was a young man and was doing market research into religions, before he chose Buddhism, he had two questions.

What is happiness?

And how do I get it?

In his talks he sometimes formulates Buddha's four noble truths as follows:

1) There is happiness
2) The cause of happiness
3) Sometimes we are unhappy
4) Why we are sometimes unhappy

Joy and Sorrow in the Book, The Prophet, by Khalil Gibran:

Then a woman said, 'Speak to us of Joy and Sorrow'
And he answered:
Your joy is your sorrow unmasked.
And the selfsame well from which your laughter rises was oftentimes filled with your tears.
And how else can it be?
The deeper that sorrow carves into your being, the more joy you can contain.
Is not the cup that holds your wine the very cup that was burned in the potter's oven?
And is not the lute that soothes your spirit, the very wood that was hollowed with knives?
When you are joyous, look deep in your heart and you shall find it is only that which has given you sorrow that is giving you joy.
When you are sorrowful look again in your heart and you shall see that in truth you are weeping for that which has been your delight.
Some of you say, 'Joy is greater than sorrow', and others say, 'Nay, sorrow is the greater'.
But I say unto you, they are inseparable.
Together they come, and when one sits alone with you at your board, remember that the other is asleep upon your bed.
Verily you are suspended like scales between your sorrow and your joy.
Only when you are empty are you at standstill and balanced.

When the treasure-keeper lifts you to weigh his gold and his silver, needs must your joy or your sorrow rise or fall.

In Indian Philosophy, happiness falls into two distinct categories.

The first is 'sukha'. This refers to ordinary happiness, which is simply the other side of ordinary unhappiness called 'dukha'.

The second category is 'ananda', also called 'shantham'. This refers to the bliss that arises from the wisdom that leads to deep inner peace. In both Buddhism and Hinduism this is called 'Nirvana'. This type of happiness is the goal of eastern spiritual practice.

8 Ways To Live Mindfully Every Day:

1) Be aware of your surroundings. While you're walking, standing or sitting, be aware of the nature, people and architecture that surrounds you.

2) Meditate. Set aside a time each day to sit still and focus on your breathing. When thoughts arise, try to simply view thoughts as thoughts, rather than judging them as positive or negative.

3) Practice listening to others. Mindfulness can help us really listen more fully to what others are saying, by being present and attentive to their words.

4) Express kindness. Make a point of expressing gratitude and appreciation of others; this will help keep you in the present experience.

5) Be still and dedicate some time to doing nothing and just 'being'. As more of our time is filled with emails, texts, social media and entertainment, periods of silence and time alone bring respite.
6) Slow down. Try to do just one task at a time, and eat slowly taking time to appreciate the food you are feeding the body.
7) Don't sweat the small stuff. When we hold onto anxiety, it makes it more difficult to live within the moment. Allow yourself to feel your feelings, and then let them go.
8) Make everyday tasks and chores a meditation. Cooking and cleaning are often seen as drudgery, but actually they are good ways to practice mindfulness and make great daily rituals.

(This is from an article on Mindfulness in Positive News - April 2013 by Nicki Allen.)

Inner peace comes from letting go.

In the words of Ajahn Chah:
'If you let go a little, you will get a little peace.
If you let go a lot you will get a lot of peace,
If you let go completely, you will get complete peace.'

SECTION TWO:
Buddhism, Hinduism and Mystic Christianity

Part 1: A Personal Perspective

These chapters are related to my own search, and will hopefully contain information that the reader will find helpful and increase their general knowledge of the field.

In fact, what is currently available in bookshops and on the Internet amounts to a huge spiritual supermarket. There is a huge choice.

I espouse no one teacher or one teaching. I have come to believe that each of us has to engage on our personal and perhaps unique learning curve. Ultimately each of us has to stand on our own feet and become our own teacher.

If these reflections assist in the person finding their own next step, then this writing will have achieved its purpose.

I have known about Buddhism, theoretically, all my life. However I did not look into it seriously until Dukka, in the form of an adverse life event hit me big time in the Christmas of 2010. Dukka is like a crying toddler. It can't be ignored.

I began to find answers. The purpose of this piece of writing is to share with others what I found.

1. The Essence of Buddhism

The Buddha did not set himself up as a personal saviour. It is important to understand this. Believing in the Buddha, as such, will not help. The Buddha held that only each person could help themselves. Each person had to become his own personal saviour.

The whole teaching can be summarised in the four noble truths:

1) The factual existence of suffering in the world (Dukka)
2) Clinging to desire (Tanha) as the cause of suffering
3) The fact that there was a way out, a remedy
4) The nature of that remedy (The Eight Fold Path)

The Buddha's way was to encourage practical study and practical investigation into these truths. We had to understand that we suffered, had to understand why we suffered, and to test out the Buddha's remedy. See if it worked for us.

It is important to understand that 'desire' is different from 'clinging to desire'.

Buddhist teaching divides life-force drivers into three categories:

1) Sense related drivers (kama tanha)
    This relates to the physiological drivers of physical existence such as the desire to eat food, quench one's thirst, excrete, look after the needs of the body, sexuality etc.
2) The driver to get things (bhava tanha)
    This relates to the emotional/mental drivers of existence such as the wish to be happy, to feel satisfied, to seek knowledge etc
3) The driver to get rid of things (vibhava tanha)
    This again relates to the emotional/mental drivers of existence, such as the wish to get rid of anger, ignorance and other things we don't want.

There is nothing inherently wrong with any of this. It is our insight and relationship to these drivers of existence that can reduce our suffering.

Please note that for the purpose of this explanation I have used the word 'driver' instead of the word desire. Desire (tanha) is the standard word used in the Buddhist lexicon. In my view this can lead to semantic misunderstanding. Just as man cannot live without food, water and breathable air, man cannot live without drivers.

I suspect what the Buddha referred to as tanha, was our 'clinging' to these drivers.

It is beyond the scope of this short essay to say more as a reader can look up any standard book on the subject. I do not set myself up as a scholar. I invite interested readers to make their own enquiries. However the Buddhist concept of 'Arahat' or enlightened person is interesting.

So What Is Enlightenment?

Ajahn Brahm describes enlightenment as a quality of emotional maturity and not an intellectual attainment.

Ajahn Sumedho, in his booklet 'The Four Noble Truths' describes three levels of understanding of the Noble Truths. The first is factual, for instance, accepting that there is suffering in life. The second level refers to insight into suffering that comes from personal investigation and personal practice. The third level, that of an Arahat, (enlightened being), refers to a profound practical understanding of the nature of Dukka. The same three levels apply to the other three truths.

Thus an enlightened being is one who has a profound understanding of the four noble truths. Such a person understands Dukka, understands the cause of Dukka, understands the remedy and is successfully able to apply it to himself thus overcoming his personal suffering.

All of us have seen film footage of the Dalai Lama. Have you noticed that he is always smiling, always jovial and laughs a lot? All of us know that his life is not easy. He has to listen and be pastor to so many displaced Tibetans, who recount terrible stories of oppression and hardship. Do you think the Dalai Lama does not suffer? Of course he does. But the suffering is not personal. This, I believe is what enlightenment means.

2. Who is a Hindu? Who is a Buddhist?

Did you know, that the first use of the word Hindu came at the time of Alexander?

Hindus were inhabitants of Hindustan, which for Alexander and the Persians, referred to all the lands beyond the Indus River. (The River Sindhu as referred to by the Persians.) This was not unlike calling the inhabitants of the Americas (north and south) Americans.

The next definition is much more recent. In the mid nineteenth century, the British did their first population census of the Indian subcontinent. A Hindu was anybody who did not claim to be a Muslim, a Christian, or something else. So it was a term of default.

It is interesting that by this time Buddhism had virtually disappeared from India.

The word Buddhist came to be used largely by nineteenth and twentieth century western travelers through various eastern lands, such as China and South East Asia, in an attempt to describe the religious beliefs of these peoples.

3. Buddha as the Tenth Avatar of Vishnu

Many believe that had Buddhism survived in India it would have been regarded as a part of the Hindu world rather like Jainism. Hindu scholars that I have spoken to have said that they had never met a Hindu who did not regard the Buddha as a Hindu and pointed out that the fact that, in popular belief, he is regarded as the Tenth Avatar of Vishnu, Lord of Dharma.

Swami Vivekananda (the disciple of Ramakrishna) who is sometimes called 'The Monk of India' regarded the Buddha as his role model.

4. Buddhism outside the shores of India

Wherever it went, Buddhism merged with the pre-existing beliefs and practices of those countries. To explore this phenomenon from a geographical, historical, political and social point of view, I found the most useful resource to be Google.

Type Buddhism Tibet, Buddhism China, Buddhism Japan, Buddhism Korea, for example and read on. It is fascinating and informative.

The BBC documentary, Seven Wonders of the Buddhist World by Bettany Hughes, is superb. See it on You Tube.

5. Buddhist Meditation

I have never personally been on a Buddhist Meditation retreat.

My own grounding in this area has been by my association with the Gurdjieff Teaching in London. My own approach to this field of endeavour can be found in my DVD production, Going Nowhere – Journey into the Tao. This is shown on my websites www.soulace.co.uk & www.lorenzodacosta.com

The purpose of this chapter is to highlight Ajahn Brahm's teaching on meditation.

With regard to the broad subject there is a lot of information on the Internet.

There are many Buddhist teachers of various traditions, many of who take meditation classes and lead retreats. An excellent book for background information is Jack Kornfield's 'Living Buddhist Masters'. Published in 1977, it is an excellent and really valuable account of the lives and teaching styles of several well known teachers of Southeast Asia, especially Burma, Thailand and Cambodia.

Until I heard Ajahn Brahm, I had not come across a teacher that went out of his way to direct his students to the 'effortless' approach. 'Right Effort' here denoted a search for 'being', not 'doing'.

On his retreats, the participants are put up in comfortable conditions and helped to rest really deeply, catch up on their sleep etc.

The You Tube talk 'Being No one, Going Nowhere' is a wonderful eye opener to this approach. Do watch it.

6. Anatta

Anatta, is a central concept in Buddhist thought. Look up Google and Wikipedia for pointers. But how to understand it practically?

Reading through Ajahn Sumedho's contemplation of space, in his book 'The Mind and The Way', it struck me that this was really helpful. I quote from the book. This is from a chapter called Noticing Space:

'...We can notice the space in a room. Most people probably wouldn't notice the space; they would notice the things in it—the people, the walls, the floor, and the furniture. But in order to notice the space what do we do? We withdraw our attention from the things, and bring our attention to the space. This does not mean getting rid of the things or denying the things their right to be there. It merely means not concentrating on them, not going from one thing to another.

The space in a room is peaceful. The objects in the room can excite, repel or attract, but the space has no such quality. However even though the space does not attract our attention, we can be fully aware of it, and we become aware of it when we are no longer absorbing into the objects in the room. When we reflect on the space in the room, we feel a sense of calm because all space is the same; the space around you and the space around me are no different. It is not mine; I can't say 'this space belongs to me' or 'that space belongs to you'

Space is always present. It makes it possible for us to be together, contained within a room, in a space that is limited by walls. Space is also outside the room; it contains the whole building, the whole world.

So space is not bound by objects in any way; it is not bound by anything. If we wish we can view space as limited in a room, but really space is unlimited.'

This letting go of focus on the objects of the room of the mind, the passing thoughts and feelings and letting in of the contemplation of space can be a useful pointer. But as with all things it is to be experienced and not become just another focus for the thought, another mental object.

7. One Dharma Buddhism

For seekers such as myself, and for Buddhist students from western countries and backgrounds, the cultural baggage associated with different sects of Buddhism such as Theravada, Vajrayana, Mahayana and Zen simply doesn't exist.

After all what does it matter what the so-called differences are. What is important is that we pick up ideas that help us in our twenty first century lives, reduce our personal suffering and make us feel that we are doing the best we can.

Ajahn Brahm when asked about the difference between different 'Buddhism's' has described them as the 'same cake with different icings'.

Many of the most respected teachers in the western world such as Jack Kornfield, Joseph Goldstein, Robert Thurman and so many others are all in favour of an integrated approach. This is being embraced by and large by all new students of Buddhism from western and even eastern backgrounds. Today the best teachers and teachings are available perhaps only via the Internet.

So perhaps the Internet will become the next monastery, the next hall of learning.

8. Ten Pali Words

Introduction to Buddhism in Ten Pali Words:

Buddha - This refers to the historical personage or to the concept of enlightenment he represents.

Dukkha - This term suggests a basic un-satisfactoriness pervading all life forms, due to the fact that all forms of life are constantly changing. This is experienced as a sense that things never measure up to our expectations and standards. Even happy and fortunate material circumstances are regarded as dukkha, as these only represent the other side of unhappy and unfortunate circumstances.

Dhamma - This refers to the factual experience and truth of 'things as they are'. All physical, emotional and mental phenomena arise and cease.

Anicca - refers to Impermanence. All mental, emotional and physical phenomena are in a state of unending flux, unending 'work in progress'

Samsara - Slavery to the pleasure-pain principle. This is the common fate and state of all persons who experience the world as dukkha.

Avijja - Personal ignorance of the laws of nature leading to life in the land of samsara and dukkha.

Nibbana - Freedom from the pleasure pain principle. The enjoyment of peace and happiness that does not depend on external circumstances. This is the goal of Buddhist life.

Magga - The path of enlightenment as taught by the Buddha. The Buddha did not teach Buddhism. He taught Magga and Dhamma.

Kamma - The operation of the law of cause and effect. Simplistic notions are best avoided. Watch this fantastic YouTube talk: Kamma without Belief by Ajahn Brahm.

Anatta - The teaching on 'non-self'. This is a central concept but complex. See Google and Wikipedia.

Pali is a derivative of the Sanskrit language in which the Buddhist scriptures were written.

Part 2: Seven Messages Of The Bhagavad-Gita

Introduction

The Bhagavad-Gita is the gospel of Hinduism and one of the great religious classics of the world. It is a very small part of a much larger work, The Mahabharata, which happens to be the longest epic poem in the world. The Gita is an exposition of the Vedanta philosophy, which is based on a very definite picture of the universe.

It is not a long book. The Christopher Isherwood translation produced in 1944 under the auspices of the Vedanta Society of Southern California, which I am familiar with, takes less than 3 hours to read. It is a conversation between two mythological beings on the edge of a battlefield. It is the most popular religious scripture of Hindu India.

Ever since I encountered it nearly forty years ago, it has been my personal bible and on the spiritual path, the love of my life.

In these seven reflections, I have endeavoured to distil some of its message.

1. The Spiritual Crisis of Arjuna

The Bhagavad-Gita Gita starts with two words. Dharmakshetre and Kurukshetre.

The blind king Dhitarasthra asks Sanjaya: "Tell me Sanjaya what my sons and the sons of Pandu did when they gathered on the field of Kurukshetre eager for battle."

Thus starts the Gita, this sacred dialogue that is to the Hindus what the Sermon on the Mount is to the Christians. Arjuna is about to embark on a battle where he is pitted against his kith and kin. He is about to be party to the slaughter of part of his own family. He is confused. He turns to Krishna.

Whether or not this historical battle actually took place, the devout Hindu, exemplified by Mahatma Gandhi, looked on what Krishna had to say as a definitive guide as to what he himself should do.

For many spiritual seekers the Gita story is an allegory of the spiritual life not unlike John Bunyan's 'The Pilgrim's Progress'.

So what is Dharmakshetre? It refers to the field of Dharma (doing the right thing).

What is Kurukshetre? It refers to the battlefield of life.

The question comes down to: 'How do I do the right thing in the battlefield of my life?'. This age old question has been at the forefront of spiritual seekers from before the time of the Buddha to the present day.

So who is a spiritual seeker?

Are you a spiritual seeker? If you want to know, ask yourself this question.

How much time do I emotionally invest into the deep questions of life?

Questions such as Who am I? Where am I going? Why? What is this life?

Keep these answers to yourself.

'Seek and you shall find. Knock and it shall be opened to you'. Familiar words?

2. Sadhana

Sadhana means the spiritual path.

Arjuna is confused. He is on the eve of a battle where his own blood relatives will face death by his hand. How can this be right? What is wrong and right?

Krishna explains that in order to understand what 'doing the right thing' means one had to discover what 'being the right person' was.

In chapter ten and eleven of the Gita, Arjuna is granted the vision of Krishna in his divine form. Arjuna is shown the resplendent, manifold universe and sees his place in it. Then he understands. He is shown the meaning of the Divine Play. The Leela.

But how can this relate to us minute, unimportant, limited beings?

What is our sadhana?

Perhaps we are only as minute, unimportant and limited as we see ourselves.

We are called upon to make our own efforts according to our own scale in the scheme of things. Yoga, in the Gita, can be regarded as a dynamic tension between doing the right thing, (the concept of dharma ruled by God Vishnu) and being the right person (the concept of the yogi ruled by the God Shiva).

3. Yoga's of the Gita

In today's world the word yoga can have many meanings. Anything from a keep-fit class, to a technique or philosophy of some sort, to a full-blown system of knowledge.

In the Gita the word yoga refers to 'The Path that leads to God'. The word for God is Brahman, in the Gita. Atman is another word meaning the same.

The Gita has eighteen chapters. Many of these are called the yoga of this or the yoga of that. The content of the chapters do not reflect the titles as such.

There are only three yoga's in the Gita, which are inseparable from each other, rather like the sides of a triangle.

They are:

1) Gyana Yoga

This is called The Yoga of Knowledge. Although sometimes mistaken for a mental path it actually refers to an Understanding of the Nature of God as is revealed to 'the eye of the mystic'. It should not be confused with book knowledge.

2) Bhakti Yoga

This is called The Yoga of Devotion. It is often confused with devotional practices such as ritual chanting, prayers, lighting candles, burning incense sticks, puja, idol worship, etc, etc. You get the picture.

However if you actually study the gita, this kind of stuff is hardly mentioned.

Bhakti Yoga refers to the opening of the heart to the Nature of God and in particular to opening the heart to the Love of God.

3) Karma Yoga

This is the path of action in the world. Over seventy percent of the Gita deals with this topic. It discusses the path of disentangled participation, where the yogi is more concerned with doing the right thing, trying to be the right person and 'come from the right place'. This consideration should override the pursuit of private goal and personal ambition.

The yogi in the Gita, as exemplified by Arjuna, opens to these three paths simultaneously. This attitude lifts him like a raft over the slaughter on the battlefield of Kurukshetra.

4) Chitta Vriti Nirodha

This is how Patanjali described yoga. Chitta means Consciousness or Mind.

Vritti means modification. Nirodha means to stop.

So Patanjali in his sutras described the path of yoga as 'stopping the modifications of the mind'.

In Sanskrit there is a saying that goes as follows: 'the mind is man's best friend. It is also his worst enemy'.

The essence of the Buddhist teaching is also about the nature of the mind. When the mind is seen for what it is, it loses its power to delude. It becomes subservient to a higher entity.

It ceases its restless roaming and becomes still. It leans towards nirvana.

Nirvana is a Sanskrit word that appears many times in the dialogue of Krishna in the Gita. It is described in the Gita as 'the peace beyond passion' and means exactly the same in the Gita as what it means in Buddhism. Indeed in essence the two teachings are one.

5) The Breaking of the Contact with Pain

In the Gita, Krishna describes yoga as that path by which the yogi breaks his/her contact with pain. What is this path? It is no different from what Buddha taught.

The following extract is taken from chapter two. I quote from the Christopher Isherwood 1945 translation. (Stanza 54 to 72)

Arjuna: Krishna, how can one identify a man who is firmly established and absorbed in Brahman? In what manner does an illumined soul speak? How does he sit? How does he walk?

Sri Krishna:
He knows bliss in the Atman
And wants nothing else.
Cravings torment the heart:
He renounces cravings.
I call him illumined.
Not shaken by adversity,
Not hankering after happiness:
Free from fear, free from anger,
Free from the things of desire.
I call him a seer and illumined.
The bonds of his flesh are broken.
He is lucky, and does not rejoice:
He is unlucky and does not weep.
I call him illumined.
The tortoise can draw in his legs:
The seer can draw in his senses.
I call him illumined.

The abstinent run away from what they desire
But carry their desires with them:
When a man enters Reality,
He leaves his desires behind him.
Even a mind that knows the path
Can be dragged from the path:
The senses are so unruly.
But he controls the senses
And recollects the mind.
And fixes it on me.
I call him illumined.
Thinking about sense-objects
Will attach you to sense-objects;
Grow attached and you become addicted;
Thwart your addiction, it turns to anger;
Be angry and you confuse your mind;
Confuse your mind, you forget the lesson of
experience;
Forget experience, you lose discrimination;
Lose discrimination, and you miss life's only purpose.
When he has no lust, no hatred,
A man walks safely among the things of lust and
hatred.
To obey the Atman
In his peaceful joy:
Sorrow melts
Into that clear peace:
His quiet mind
Is soon established in peace.
The uncontrolled mind
Does not guess the Atman is present:
How can it meditate?
Without meditation, where is peace?

Without peace, where is happiness?
The wind turns a ship
From its course upon the waters:
The wandering winds of the senses
Cast man's mind adrift
And turn his better judgement from its course.
When a man can still the senses
I call him illumined.
The recollected mind is awake
In the knowledge of the Atman
Which is dark night to the ignorant:
The ignorant are awake in their sense-life
Which they think is daylight:
To the seer it is darkness.
Water flows continually into the ocean
But the ocean is never disturbed.
Desire flows into the mind of the seer
But he is never disturbed.
The seer knows peace:
The man who stirs up his own lusts
Can never know peace.
He knows peace who has forgotten desire.
He lives without craving:
Free from ego, free from pride
This is the state of enlightenment in Brahman:
A man does not fall back from it
Into delusion.
Even at the moment of death
He is alive in that enlightenment:
Brahman and he are one.

For me this passage has summarised the essential
teaching of the Gita.

When I visited Ajahn Sumedho's monastery (Amaravati) in England, and saw how the monks there lived, they seemed to personify the teaching of Lord Krishna, as described in the Gita. For me this indicated that perfect exemplars of the teaching of the Gita were to be found in Buddhism. For me Buddha and Krishna are one.

6) Kshetrajana- Knower of The Field

Chapter thirteen of the Gita is called 'The Field and its Knower'.

Krishna describes the field as the body-mind complex where the seeds of action in this life are sown. This refers to our life where the process of living engenders the sowing of various seeds and leads to the inevitable reaping of various karmas, or fruits. The very process of life generates karmas whether we like it or not. These fruits appear either in this life or the next. Such is the teaching of Krishna. Krishna then goes on to describe the 'Knower of the Field', which is the goal of the teaching of the Gita. This 'knower' refers to the part of us that can witness our life with indifference.

This is our highest part.

In Buddhist meditation, as in meditation in other traditions, we try to open to a state of deep aware silence, where our monkey mind thoughts, our transient feelings and our changing body tensions and sensations are seen and accepted as they are.

They are seen as an indifferent witness might see it. This is the connection to our inner Krishna, the inner attractor seated in the middle of our heart, loving all, embracing all.

7) Time and Synergy

Time in the Gita is not linear but cyclical. All time is subjective and related to the creature involved. Krishna speaks of the creation and dissolution of the universe in cycles.

All time is related to breath. On a cosmic scale there is the 'Breath of Brahma'. On the level of the microcosmos, of man, of an animal or a microbe his life is like a breath. It arises and it ceases.

Krishna represents God on the level of the cosmos. Arjuna is a god among men.

The functioning of the cosmos requires this synergy between Krishna and Arjuna.

Without Krishna it cannot be done. Without Arjuna it will not be done.

So how are we to understand our inner Krishna and our inner Arjuna?

Part 3: Christianity Through Eastern Eyes

Introduction

I was born and brought up a Catholic. My mother was exceptionally religious. So Christianity as seen through the eyes of teachers of eastern religions has been important to me. I am personally very fond of religious imagery, and my 'shrine room' at home bustles with pictures and images of various deities and gurus. Pictures of Jesus and Mary hang alongside those of Buddha and Shiva. For me there is no difference between Gods and Religions. 'God' is one. The various deities are God's many faces. In the teachings of the East 'God' has two aspects, like two sides of a coin. One aspect is 'God without Name or Form'. The Hindus call this Nirguna Brahman and the Buddhists call this 'The Unborn, Unformed, and Unconditioned'.

The other aspect is 'God of Name and Form'. These are the Buddha's, Shiva's, Christ's, Marys and the pantheon of deities, saints, etc that form the focus of devotion for many people.

In the Bhagavad-Gita, Krishna says that although contemplation of God without Form is superior, this is in practice very difficult for an embodied soul to realise. Hence one has to go through God with Form. One has to find their personal god, rather like a personal guardian angel. This is called 'istha-devata'. For Christians, this will usually take the form of an image such as Christ on the

Cross, The Sacred Heart of Jesus, Mary Help of Christians or The Madonna and Baby Jesus.

1. 'The Kingdom Of Heaven Is Within You'

This quote from Luke 17:21, has been a centrepiece of the East's teaching about The Sermon on The Mount, and the essence of Jesus' message.

What is Heaven? And where is it?

Is heaven some 'physical type place', some place up there in the sky where folks play harps and live on ambrosia?

Where is it? In here or out there? Whatever 'in here' or 'out there' might mean.

From an eastern perspective, the matter is approached by opening to this question.

The manuscript called 'The Cloud of Unknowing' is an anonymous work dated to the fourteenth century. The east celebrates this as a true pointer.

What does it mean? Can this be a question for us?

No answers. The quest is to open to a question.

2. 'Be Still and Know That I Am God'

This quote from Psalm 46:10 is quoted by every eastern teacher I have come across when they are asked about Christianity. These include Ajahn Brahm and Eckhart Tolle.

And with good reason.

At the heart of Hindu and Buddhist Meditation, is the search for that space of stillness, which sits in the heart.

Surrounded by a maelstrom of our personal 'stuff', our story, our drama, our thought, our relationships, our circumstances, our life, our 'me', our 'I and mine'.

In brief moments, we glimpse it, and know…even if from afar.

We begin to glimpse 'The Knowing, The Gnosis'. But it does not belong to us.

3. Christ on the Cross

If we contemplate this familiar image, we can open to two contradictory things.

Christ on the cross is a tortured figure. Full of pain and suffering. Like our lives.

Our lives are full of pain, of 'dukka'. As the saying goes 'we have to carry our cross'.

This is how life is whether we want it or not.

Look at Christ's face again. It has a quality of radiance. The Christ risen.

The Buddha lives in both the Dukka, and in The Nirvana. Like The Christ.

Can we search for a message for ourselves in this?

4. Mary. Mother Goddess. Queen of Angels.

Our mothers give us birth. On the deepest level they are part of us in a way our fathers could never be. The father is external. The mother is internal. Mothers nurture us in the way our fathers cannot do.

In Catholic Christianity, Mary is our cosmic mother, Christ is the father figure.

In my upbringing, I was taught to pray to Mary, rather than Jesus. Things come as an act of grace, not based on justice. If Mary is pleased with you, she will ask her son Jesus Christ to grant her wish. And which son will not grant a wish of his mother?

This is the prayer to Mary:

Hail Mary, Full of Grace, The Lord is with Thee, Blessed art Thou among women and blessed is the fruit of Thy womb, Jesus. Holy Mary, Mother of God, Pray for us sinners, now, and at the hour of our deaths, Amen.

5. 'I am The Way, The Truth and The Life...'

"I am the Way and the Truth and the Life. No one comes to the father except through me." John 14:6

I have yet to come across of a 'fundamentalist Christian sect' that has not used this quote to justify why they are 'chosen' and others are either wrong or not quite chosen.

Eastern teachers, such as Paramahansa Yogananda, who claims in his world famous book 'Autobiography of a Yogi' to have actually had a personal vision and audience with Jesus Christ, has written on his interpretation of the Christian message.

What is the way? What is the truth? What is the life?

Can this be a question for us?

6. Reincarnation and Christianity

It is a well-documented fact that the ancient Greeks had beliefs about reincarnation.

In his book 'Masks of the Soul' Benjamin Walker, expertly covers the history of reincarnation theory. And Dr Raymond Moody, considered 'the father of the Near Death Experience', and whose book 'Life after Life' brought him international fame in 1975, is an expert on the beliefs of the ancient Greeks.

As Christianity took hold as a state religion, views and beliefs about reincarnation were suppressed and disenfranchised. This became Church of Rome policy in the fourth century. For scholars interested in reincarnation beliefs in Christianity, 'Masks of the Soul' is really interesting. The author quotes chapter and verse.

7. The Eastern God and the Western God

Melvyn Bragg is a well-known media personality in Britain and presenter of BBC Radio 4's 'In Our Time'. By a complete accident I happened to listen to an episode called 'The History of God'. In this hour-long programme, he interviewed various scholars who discussed the views of various notable philosophers such as Descartes on the existence or non-existence of God. What struck me was that there was no reference to the religions of the East. It was as though the non-Judeo Christian world simply did not exist. India, China, Asia were not even mentioned in passing.

Reflecting on this fact, I had an eureka moment. It struck me that until the publication of Max Mueller's 'The Sacred Writings of the East' in the latter part of the nineteenth century, western scholars and thinkers, were for all practical purposes completely ignorant of the religious beliefs of the east, about Hinduism, Buddhism and Taoism.

The argument about whether a Judaeo-Christian type creator god did or did not exist was the only show in town. The eastern concept of the inseparability of 'God' from creation was a non-topic.

Similarly in the east, Hindus, Buddhists and Taoists would have considered the concept of a separate creator god utterly strange and for them a non-topic.

Who is interested in arguing and discussing a non-topic?

8. Christianity Through The Eye Of Eastern Gurus

There is nowadays a very large literature available on the topic of Christianity as seen through the lens of Eastern teachers. Gurdjieff's pupil Dr Maurice Nicholl wrote a book on the meaning of the parables in the gospels, called 'The New Man'. Jacob Needleman's book 'Lost Christianity', jostles alongside copies of 'The Cloud of Unknowing', The Gnostic Gospels' and so many other books on New Age bookshops. In my generation, Watkins Bookshop (possibly the oldest esoteric bookshop in the western world) in Leicester Square in London has been a Mecca for 'students' such as myself. The bookshop staff are an excellent source of information on the plethora of books on esoteric Christianity.

Part 4: Buddhist Psychology and the Game of Life - A Personal Perspective

Introduction

Strictly speaking the term Buddhist Psychology refers to counseling and psychotherapy principles as expounded by authors such as The Dalai Lama, Alan Watts, Tara Brach, Jack Kornfield, Joseph Goldstein, Sharon Salzberg, Pema Chodron, Mark Epstein and others who are highly respected teachers in today's Buddhism, particularly in America and Europe.

However, as I see it, the essential teachings of Buddhism predate the Buddha and can be found in the teachings of Lao Tzu in China and in the schools of Advaita Vedanta of India.

Practical approaches to understanding the philosophy and practice of the Tao can be found in the books, workshops, and video interviews of such teachers as Wayne Dyer and Barefoot Doctor (Stephen Russell)

Practical approaches to the philosophy and practice of Advaita Vedanta (Non Dualism) can be found in the books, workshops and video interviews of teachers such as Adyashanti and Jeff Foster.

It is important to remember that outside the proverbial 'east' these ideas can also be found in the philosophies and beliefs of the ancient Greeks and Romans with respect to their teachings on Stoicism and in the writings of western philosophers such as Baruch de Spinoza.

However I wish to approach this subject practically, and am using the term 'Buddhist psychology' as an umbrella term that includes The Tao and Vedanta. I propose to look at certain common principles and point to how they may be applied to what I am calling 'The Game of Life'.

1. The Game of Life

So what is this 'Game of Life'? It refers to the personal narrative that each living person is, moment by moment, and day-by-day constructing for themselves about how they are interacting with the forces of life, the forces of society and the forces of the environment as they subjectively experience them. This will always be a mixture of thoughts and emotions. This is obvious to us, from the moment we wake in the morning to the time we sleep at night. This mechanism probably persists when we are asleep though we are not aware of it.

This 'narrative' is equally present when everything is going 'swimmingly well' and one feels 'on top of the world' to the other extreme when things have gone 'horribly wrong' to the point that one feels that 'life is not worth living'. And everything in between.

Where is this located? And why is this important?

The experience of the 'game of life is located in the front of the psychic field.

I do not subscribe to the idea that our 'mind' is located in our brain, or in the cranium.

Our brain as an organ is simply like a radio apparatus that allows us to tune into the function of our mind, which has a personal component as well as a non-personal component, which is part of what we sometimes call the 'Universal Mind'.

This situation is not unlike the functioning of our personal computers and the Internet.

Many of us no longer store our data in our PCs. We transfer data storage to companies such as Google who as far as we are concerned have their servers in the sky. From these 'data clouds in the sky' we can access what we need, when we need through our PCs. So our brain is like our PC and our mind is like the 'data bank in the sky'. If our brain is damaged by disease such as a stroke or Alzheimer's, our ability to access our mind is impaired, like a defective PC. When our PC breaks down we can throw it away and get a replacement. This can sadly not be done with our brain.

There are possibly several systems that localise functions in the human psychic field, i.e. the space contained in the human aura, which extends a few inches beyond the skin.

There is the Chakra system for instance consisting of seven points from the base of the spine to the top of the head.

I personally prefer the system expounded by the Russian mystic G I Gurdjieff, which has always made complete practical sense to me. Gurdjieff described seven 'centres', five 'lower centres/functions' and two 'higher centres/functions'.

The five 'lower functions/minds' that concern us are:
1) The thinking mind located in the head area
2) The feeling mind located in the chest area
3) The external movement mind located in the low back area

4) The internal organ mind located in the abdominal area
5) The sex function mind located in the pelvic area

It is beyond the scope of this essay to go into more detail. Interested readers can consult 'The Psychology of Man's Possible Evolution' and 'In Search of The Miraculous' both by P D Ouspensky for detailed information on psycho-physiology of Gurdjieff's System. However it is straightforward to understand that when a person says 'I think' they point to their forehead. When they say 'I feel' they point to their heart area. We know that sexual orgasm is experienced in the pelvis.

Try walking across the room. Try and sense where the centre of gravity of this physical command originates. Is it not in the low back?

Why is this location important?

The game of life narrative is experienced in the front of the psychic field, just in front of the forehead and face. This is the area where the human organism processes incoming sensory and other information and raw data from the outside world.

Try and sense this for yourself.

The seat of wisdom, imagination, long term plans, religious thinking, and so on are located in the back of the upper psychic field, in the area of the crown of the head.

We even use the term 'the back of the mind' to signify exactly this. We say 'at the back of my mind I had this thought, this aim, this idea...' Try and sense this.

Accessing the 'Back Of The Mind'

1. Mindfulness and Awareness

This forms the backbone of various Buddhist, Taoist and Yoga approaches.

In Vipassana (Insight Meditation) practice for instance, one allows oneself to 'fall into' the sensation of the physical body, into the sensation of breathing, to ground oneself in the experience of the present moment. One simultaneously opens oneself to seeing ones thoughts and feelings come and go, emphatically without trying to comment on them or modify them. In various traditions, this activity is called 'witnessing'. It is this witnessing of the activity of the mind that provides the wisdom insights. It is beyond the scope of this essay to discuss this further but suffice to say that this endeavour takes many years. There is an extensive literature on this subject and it forms the basis of many 'dhamma talks' that can be accessed on YouTube and the Internet.

The Martial Arts, Hatha Yoga, The Gurdjieff Movements & Tai Chi

Practices like Tai Chi, Chi Gong, Yoga postures, Buddhist Walking for example have an outer form and an inner form. The outer form can be seen in live demonstrations or in video form on the Internet.

The inner form, which from the point of view of the back of the mind is the important bit, is very subtle. It involves the cultivation of present moment awareness through the precise sensation and execution of specific outer movements, like a dance form, whilst simultaneously working on the cultivation of attention. This is an exceptionally useful approach to certain types of people.

An appropriate teacher is probably essential at least in the beginning.

I recall a well-respected Tai Chi teacher in the UK in the 1990s being asked about the essence of his practice. He answered very simply 'Tai Chi is the art of transferring the weight of the body from one foot to the other'. Profound?

In the Zen tradition, profundity and simplicity are, dare I say it, the same.

Aspects of the Game of Life

On a practical level, each human being has three interlocking, yet separate spheres of engagement with the forces of life. We do not ask (or perhaps we do) to be born into the human realm, but once born we are subject to these aspects whether we like it or not.

1) **The me-me sphere**. This sphere pertains to what is utterly personal to you and cannot be shared even with your nearest and dearest. This includes your body, your personal health, and your deepest innate drives and longings. For example if you suffer from migraine headaches, no matter how much your family and work colleagues support you, it is you and only you that has to experience the headache.

2) **The sphere of family and friends.** This is your emotional family, which includes your pets. In this

sphere you will experience happy times and triumphs as well as sad times and disasters.

3) **The sphere of work.** All of us, or most of us, have to find a way to earn a living to put bread on our table. We can on average spend a third of our lives on this. As a rule of thumb we spend a third of our life working, a third of our life socialising and a third of our lives sleeping. In this sphere of interaction as well we will experience our triumphs and disasters.

The Stark Choice

All human beings from kings and queens, to down-and-out persons are equally subject to the game of life be it bitter or sweet. There are no exceptions.

Those folks who, for one reason or another become aware, that they do not have to submit to becoming hapless victims of their inner narrative about external events, that there is another way, another possibility, can become spiritual seekers.

So who is a spiritual seeker and why do they become one?

My experience of life has revealed that spiritual seeking has little to do with education, money or social status. The bulk of medical colleagues I have come across in my working life have displayed no interest in this kind of thing.

I am now of the opinion that, this kind of activity and interest has to be part of your karma, part of what you bring with you into this life, part of something very innate, part of the me, me sphere of the aspect of the

Game of Life. But I could be wrong and hope I'm wrong.

Pillars of Buddhist Psychology for the Spiritual Seeker

Impermanence

Everything is moving, changing, morphing. All states are unstable. Nothing stays the same for long. This is Anicca in Buddhist terminology, In the Tao there is the play between Yin and Yang, the I-Ching is translated as the Book of Changes. Nothing is really at rest. In Vedanta there is the eternal play of the forces of Dwaita (duality), this duality overplayed by the three mutable forces of Rajas (active), Tamas (passive) and Sattwa (reconciling). This system itself again is inexorably moving through the cycle of birth, life death and rebirth-like some kind of spiral in perpetual motion.

Only one thing is stable, the principle of change. You can set your watch on one thing, the fact that the time will change.

When we are having a good time it seems to go very quickly. When things are difficult, when times are hard it feels like it is going to last forever. In understanding impermanence, we understand that it won't. All we need to do is to be patient and wait. Ajahn Brahm has composed this teaching story about life. The person is likened to a passenger in a bus that is winding its way through the road of life. The bus goes through beautiful countryside with meadows, green forests, lakes and waterfalls, beautiful wild flowers growing by the wayside. And the person shouts to the driver 'slow down, I want to enjoy this' but the bus seems to speed up and race along and all of a sudden the bus enters a different area, no longer beautiful countryside but more like a toxic dump. The earth seems scorched, trees stunted, garbage everywhere, everything looks hideous and the person shouts at the driver 'speed up, get a move on, I want to get out of here'. But instead the bus feels like its slowing down to a crawl.

The person gets out of his seat to find the driver and remonstrate with him for not obeying orders. When the person gets to the driver's compartment he discovers that there's no one there. It is a driverless bus. What to do? There is only one thing to do.

The person goes back to their seat, sits down, shuts up and stops complaining. After all there is no one to complain to. The person realises that there is nothing to do but allow the bus to wind its way out of the countryside that feels like a toxic dump. One waits for the light at the end of the tunnel. It has to be there. The toxic dump can't last forever. Nothing does.

Difficulties

For most people life is difficult. Unforeseen and un-summoned difficulties turn up like unwanted guests in our me-me sphere, our family and friends sphere and our work sphere. And we have to deal with these unwanted guests who rob us of our peace and at times turn our lives upside down.

This is what brings most people to search on the spiritual path and look for a meaning to their lives and find a way to relate to their difficulties.

All religions, all spiritual teachers address this precise issue.

Within eastern traditions they say that working through difficulties in a positive fashion, considering difficulties as opportunities to learn and grow, and finding a way to 'convert base metals into gold' to use a term from alchemy is what this life on the earthly plane is about. They say that if life had no difficulties then this would be like a broad paved road going nowhere.

The choice for spiritual seekers is between victimhood and engagement.

'Eat or be eaten' is one of Gurdjieff's sayings.

Control

A vast amount of stress is generated by the drive to control aspects of life over which we have little or no control. In relation to ourselves, our family and friends and our workplace it is as though life happens while we are busy making other plans. And this stresses us out. If stress is prolonged this leads to depression, anxiety and loss of energy. This impacts on our personal health and also on our family and workplace.

What to do? Well, we have to gain insight into the laws of life and the flow of life.

We have to learn to 'Let go' and as the Tao says become like water and go with the flow.

Attitudes

All the gurus tell us that working on changing our attitudes from self centered and egocentric to non-self centered and non-egocentric is perhaps the most powerful spiritual tool for transformation. For example, changing ones attitude from 'what's in it for me?' To 'How can I help.'

Social Capital

In the UK there are TV programs like Location, Location, Location.

They promote the idea that money can buy you a happy home.

What rubbish. A happy home consists of a collection of happy people who are focused on helping each other and the folks they come in contact with. This kind of happiness cannot be bought with money. We have to remember that when we are very young, very old or very sick we cannot survive without being looked after. This care is usually provided by family and friends and cannot be paid for in money.

Creating financial capital is important, but creating social capital is even more important. So instead of thinking location, location, location, think people, people, people.

Other Areas

There are several more areas but this has been covered in the 'letting go' sections.

2. The Search For Guidance

For those that feel drawn to the search, it becomes clear that they need to put themselves under the influence of a teacher or teaching. Baring rare exceptions, the average person cannot expect to get anywhere without help. In this sense, spiritual development is not unlike going to medical school, engineering school, music school or painting school. It takes hard slog over many years to even develop an aim.

Accomplished Buddhist monks for instance will tell you that it took them years of hard slog to develop their insights. Many evolved persons I have come across have told me that it is their opinion that there are no shortcuts, no easy way. However it is probably essential to try out supposed short cuts and easy ways as part of one's learning curve

But as the Chinese proverb goes…'The journey of a thousand miles begins with a single step'. It is all right to have a big picture or a big aim but what becomes obvious is that the only important step is the next one. It is helpful to remember the saying … 'Rome was not built in a day'.

Finding a Guide

When I started my search some forty years ago the world was a very different place. Information was scanty and hard to access. The Internet did not exist. The odd book and the odd person were the only resources then available.

For seekers starting off today it is like a different planet. The Internet has made it possible for people to be literally drowning in information. One no longer has to search in the fastness of the Himalayas for words and teachings of a wise guide.

Google and YouTube bring the Himalayas to you. There is a vast choice. It is fantastic. Why travel a large distance to sit at the back of a crowded room, straining to hear a famous teacher speak. If the talk is audio taped or videoed you can watch this in the comfort of your own home at a time to suit you.

Market Research

In my opinion the Watkins 100 list is one of the most useful contributions to modern spirituality. Started in 2011 by Etan Ilfeld, Editor in chief of the quarterly Watkins Review, it is a list of the 100 outstanding people in the field of Spirituality.

Prospective seekers can Google the names, read their Wikipedia entries and hone their search to individuals that most appeal to their needs and what they are looking for.

I used to think I had a very good general knowledge until I saw the list and discovered how much I had not come across. www.batgap.com and www.conscious.tv are other fabulous resources.

Gurus with feet of clay

In my opinion seekers should not worry about this. The guru that is most likely to help you is likely to be a human being like you are. The fact that such a person eats meat, drinks alcohol, smokes and womanises (male gurus), does not detract from what they may have to offer. My own guru of 25 years, Gurdjieff had a 'terrible reputation', yet he is also undoubtedly one of the greatest gurus of the twentieth century. When Bill Clinton had his well publicised problems in the White House he had tremendous support from Americans that said they were unconcerned about personal moral issues as they had elected a president, not a pope, and as such they were concerned with his management of the economy and not his personal peccadilloes.

Is it better to learn something from the devil instead of worshipping an angel on a pedestal but learn nothing?

At the end of the day the seeker has to find their own way and become their own guru.

Perhaps the way to approach this is to cultivate the attitude of separating the wheat from the chaff, and taking from various gurus, books, talks etc, what is applicable and relevant to one at the time. Common sense can be the guiding principle.

Satsang

This is an Indian term meaning 'spiritual company'. In common parlance, in India this refers to social meetings of groups of people where only spiritual things (as opposed to mundane things) are discussed.

For spiritual seekers to find kindred spirits is essential. A group of people can achieve what a single individual cannot. There is also another side. On the long and winding spiritual road there are highs and lows. When one is going through a low period, the support of one's spiritual family is so valuable. And one reciprocates by being there for others in their time of need.

The use of the Internet now allows the possibility of finding a satsang group on the net. Many such groups exist. So geographic closeness is no longer a necessity.

3. Facing our Fears

Underneath the surface, we can see that we are a bundle of worries and fears.

Almost all our fears are about only two things:

1) We fear we may lose what we already have.
2) We fear that we may not get what we want.

We can see that, these fears generate a level of anxiety that rob us of any deep peace of mind. As we gain insight into the mechanisms that keep us either overtly or subliminally, in a state of chronic worry, fear and anxiety, it becomes clearer to us that peace of mind is actually the highest happiness.

The Buddha's teaching on this was actually quite simple. He asked his followers to investigate for themselves the level of control they truly had over their external environment and over external events. They would discover that it was very little.

This being the case, people could not meaningfully protect what they already had from loss. They were equally powerless to ensure they 'got what they wanted'.

Trying to protect what you cannot protect and achieve what you cannot achieve is an exercise in futility and will simply leads to stress and a sense of failure.

The Buddha suggested that the wise way to live was to understand the laws of nature and submit to the laws of nature. Everything is uncertain. We have to understand that this uncertainty has to be accepted, embraced and lived with. This is life's supreme reality. If we imagine this reality to be a person, the choice facing us is for us to either invite this person to come and live with us as a welcome guest or face the fact that if we do not do that, this person will force themselves into our house and live with us as an unwanted guest. Another way of putting this is as follows: 'You may as well embrace the reality of your life because if you don't the reality of your life will embrace you'.

The Buddha taught that the way to face life was to live in the present moment.

Happiness was forthcoming when we learned to be kind to ourselves, kind to others and kind to our environment. Being mindful and kind...being 'kindful', (Ajahn Brahm often uses this word).

All of us will go through difficult times. This is guaranteed.

The choice we have is with what attitude we face this.

In the words of Dr Wayne W Dyer:

'With everything that has happened to you, you can either feel sorry for yourself or treat what has happened to you as a gift. Everything is either an opportunity to grow or an obstacle to keep you from growing. You get to choose'.

4. Saturn

In Indian Astrology (Jyotish) Saturn (Shani) is considered to be the most important of the planets. Its placement in your horoscope will to a large extent determine the difficulties and troubles you will face in your life. In worst-case scenarios it is nothing less than a harbinger of doom. Much of Indian Astrology is connected with finding ways to placate the influence of Saturn in a person's life. In Indian Astrology, even the deities (gods and goddesses) are subject to the influence of Saturn. So all human beings will go through astrologically determined periods of stress, trouble and loss. How they weather these difficult climatic periods to some extent is in their hands.

In the summer 2013 edition of Watkins Review, there is a wonderful interview with Eckhart Tolle. Two things stood out for me:

1) 'Life is difficult'...these are the starting words of the once international bestseller, The Road Less Travelled by M Scott Peck. Eckhart agreed that

these were probably the most famous first lines ever written.

2) When asked his view on the purpose of life on earth his reply included the sentences... 'The world isn't here to make us happy, but to make us conscious. Comfort and security are not part of the ultimate purpose of the universe. ....'

Let us look at the leading lights among the spiritually influential people today. These include Eckhart Tolle, The Dalai Lama, Dr Wayne Dyer, Thich Nhat Hanh, Deepak Chopra, Louise Hay, Ken Wilber, Byron Katie and many, many others.

A common theme that emerges from what they have to say is that inner growth comes from engaging with the inevitable difficulties in life in a positive way. This will include cultivating a positive and optimistic outlook, learning how to develop positive thinking, and cultivating a compassionate heart open to the difficulties of others, being of help to others and learning how to forgive both others and ourselves in relation to issues from the past.

We cultivate the understanding that the purpose of forgiveness is not to help others but to help ourselves. We cannot really help others till we learn to help ourselves.

Saturn as our Guru

Can we embrace the difficulties in life as our guru of the moment? This financial difficulty, that relationship issue, this family spat, that health issue?

Can we say 'yes' to our difficulties?

The Four Goals of Life

The Vedic scriptures declare that this earthly life has four purposes (purusharthas)

1) Artha or the pursuit of material prosperity
2) Dharma or the pursuit of righteousness
3) Kama or the pursuit of physical and emotional pleasure
4) Moksha or the pursuit of Liberation

These make perfect sense don't they?

But I suspect not all of us are destined to achieve all these easily.

We have to work with our difficulties.

Astrology can help and so can psychics and mediums.

Saturn and Indian Astrology

Interested persons are advised to read these books:

1) Light on Life: An Introduction to Indian Astrology By Hart De Fouw and Robert V Svoboda
2) The Greatness of Saturn: A Therapeutic Myth By Robert V Svoboda

5. Journey into Spiritualism

In 2008, I encountered the phenomenon of mediumship for the first time.

I had vaguely heard of 'mediums' and 'sittings' but in July 2008, completely out of curiosity, I had a 'sitting' with a medium Henry Cumming in Richmond, London. It blew my mind.

The experience of seeing someone seemingly connect to a discarnate realm was amazing.

In 2011 after retiring from medical practice, and with time on my hands to indulge my interests, my path took me to The London Spiritual Mission, a spiritualist church in the Bayswater area of Central London, where as I was to discover they had services including demonstrations of clairvoyance three times a week.

I have by now attended about four hundred services and seen various mediums, give messages from the dead to the living.

I have to say that it has been the most amazing thing I have seen on the path of spiritual searching so far.

I have no explanation for how it works, but it does and it is there for all to see.

I have not come across a single fake or charlatan, though no doubt some must exist.

I have myself received a most convincing message from my dear mother who died in 2007.

It is beyond the scope of this piece of writing to say anything about the Spiritualist Movement, but I would encourage spiritual seekers to attend spiritualist services, see mediums at work, and then make up their mind for themselves. It may not be everyone's cup of tea. Try to keep an open mind.

For folks who have no previous exposure but want to get a flavour of what's it about go to YouTube and look up names like James Van Praagh, Tony Stockwell, Colin Fry, Gordon Smith and Lisa Williams. Also look up publications such as 'Psychic News' and 'Two Worlds'.

To get a broad flavour of the types of activities offered under the Spiritualist umbrella do look up the website of The College of Psychic Studies, London. By and large demonstrations of clairvoyance to the public, are confined to Britain, the USA and a few other places in the western world. Nothing like this can be found in India, China, Japan, Asia and most other parts of the world.

6. Evidence Based Religion

I have come across only two evidence-based religions Buddhism and Spiritualism. However these are evidence based for quite different reasons. Buddhism is evidence based because it does not require belief in 'a higher power'. It focuses on the fact of suffering in ordinary life and the cause and 'cure' for this. It requires personal investigation and testing of the theory.

Although Buddhism teaches about 'reincarnation' this is not an essential teaching at all. Buddhist monks like Ajahn Sumedho have replied to questions like 'What happens after death?' with the reply ' How should I know as I haven't died yet!'

Spiritualism is evidence based, as the stated aim of clairvoyant demonstrations is to demonstrate that there is no death as such. The personality of the dead person simply goes into 'another room' and they can be contacted. The purpose of the demonstrations is to provide evidence of this.

Having personally witnessed at least 400 clairvoyant demonstrations within church settings, I am now convinced of this fact, although I have no explanation for the phenomenon.

FURTHER INFORMATION

In 2007, I began to experience curious dreams. They would typically start at about 2 am and last till about 3.30am. In these dreams I invariably saw myself as a classroom teacher in front of an old fashioned blackboard, trying to make a complex subject simple to students who appeared as a shadowy group. The dreams occurred 7 days a week and gave me no peace. I was at the time working as a GP Doctor putting in 60-70 hours a week, I not only had to see patients but also run the practice, which at the time employed 8 people. In July 2008 strolling through Richmond Town Centre on my lunch break, I came across an announcement in a shop window about private sittings with medium Henry Cumming. Without prior intent I found myself seeing Henry for a sitting. Henry said that his 'spirit guides' were informing him that I was destined to author a mind, body, spirit product which would go far and wide and help many people.

My dreams suddenly made sense, and directed me to an audiovisual product rather than a conventional book, I found myself drawing some 150 slides in a period of 6 weeks. It became clear that I would have to find someone with IT skills to develop this project. Bumping into Henry again, I asked him about this. "You will meet the person in this very shop". A fortnight later I met Tim Lee at the very place mentioned. He turned out to be an artist with IT skills. I discussed the conversation with Henry and he agreed to take on the job. Both our lives went through a period of great difficulty and it was not until the Christmas period of 2009 when the DVDs were recorded, essentially, in one take, in the evenings using a vacant room at my GP Surgery. The moment the recordings were finished, it was as though a great weight came off my back, and I could not remember anything.

Looking back now I have no idea of how such a large assortment of information coalesced and organised itself through my faculties. I could certainly not do it again.

In the DVD set I describe aspects of my own personal journey in relation to the ideas and information in the lectures.

Contents of the 4 DVD's

DVD 1. Meditation:

1. What is Consciousness?

2. What is Meditation?

3. Overview of methods. Trying to listen. Trying to do.

4. Awareness. Sensory Awareness.

5. 'Be here now'

6. Why Meditate?

7. Achieve What?

8. The How. Four primary practices.

9. a. Sensing the breath

   b. Sensing the body

   c. Observing thoughts and feelings

   d. Deepening sense impressions

10. Observing thoughts and feelings. The theory of Inner Freedom. Witness states. The Practice.

11. Energies and Functions. Modalities of experience. Thought mechanism. Associations. External movement. Sex function. Internal metabolism. Habitual thoughts, feelings and postures. Sitting still.

12. The Law of Thirds. Head, heart and body knowledge. The concept of Harmonious Man

13. Concluding comments where to look.

DVD 2. Mysticism

1. The issue of context. Mysticism in context

2. Theology and Gnosticism. Organised and personal religion

3. Contrasting the Traditions. Judeo – Christian (The West), Hindu/Buddhist/Taoist (The East), Concept of 'God', 'Reality' 'This Life' 'Good and Evil' How they differ.

4. The Vedic World. The Sanskrit heritage. Systems of philosophy (including Buddhism.)A backdrop to concepts that follow.

5. The Vedic Universe. Non-Phenomenal Existence. Four thought experiments.

6. The Vedic Universe. Phenomenal Existence, Unity, Duality, Triads, Change and Impermanence

7. Non-Phenomenal Existence. The Human Experience.

8. Yoga. Yoga today. Classical Yoga. Yoga of the Bhagavad-Gita. Does Yoga prolong life?

9. Karma and Reincarnation. Basic ideas and where to look for information about Indian Karmic Theory.

10. Death and Dying. What is on the other side? Death and dying in the mystical traditions

11. Science and Religion

12. Unity in Mysticism. How west and east say the same thing.

DVD 3. Medicine

1. The Medicine -Metaphysics Interface. The Maslow Hierarchy Diagram

2. Is Orthodox Medicine holistic?

3. The Alternative (CAM)/Orthodox Medicine divide

4. Spiritual perspectives in Orthodox Medicine. Are there any?   Talking Therapies

5. Interesting Studies

    a Emotional Intelligence – Daniel
    Goleman

    b Neuroplasticity – Dr Richard
    Davidson

    c Happiness Research – Dr Martin Seligman

    d The Faith Gene – Dr Dean Hamer

    e The Chemistry of Emotions – Dr Candace
    Pert

    f Hierarchy of Needs – Abraham Maslow

    g Transactional Analysis – Eric Berne

    h Rogerian Counseling – Carl Rogers

6. Mind-Body Medicine as an adjunct to other therapies

7. Movement as Therapy. Reichian Therapy. Bioenergetics.   Posture and movement techniques

8. Mindfulness techniques in therapy

9. Transpersonal approaches to therapy

10. The 'Unconscious' in therapy. The concept of The Unconscious Freud – Freudian Psychoanalysis, Jung – Jungian Analysis, Assagioli -Transpersonal Psychology, Weiss – Past Life

Regression Therapy Meditation Practice and The Unconscious

11. Past Life Regression Therapy. Dr Brian Weiss and others

12. Will evidence for past lives herald the next great epoch of study

DVD 4. Books

Introduction to the selection

1. Autobiography of a Yogi – Paramahansa Yogananda

2. G.I.Gurdjieff

    a In Search of the Miraculous – P.D.Ouspensky

    b Meetings with Remarkable Men – G.I.Gurdjieff

    c Gurdjieff Memoirs – Fritz Peters

3. The Buddhist Masters:

    a The Dalai Lama

    b Thich Nhat Hanh

    c Ajahn Sumedho

d Jack Kornfield

e Soygal Rinpoche – The Tibetan book of Living and Dying

4. Eckhart Tolle and Krishnamurti

5. The Aghora Trilogy – Robert Svoboda

   a At the Left Hand of God

   b Kundalini

   c The Law of Karma

6. Swami Rama – Living with the Himalayan MastersLiving with a Himalayan Master – Justin O'Brien

7. Paul Brunton:

   a A Search in Secret India

   b A Search in Secret Egypt

8. John Bennett, Witness. Bennett's research into the Parousia (New Age) Sri Yukteshwar's Yuga computation 1898

9. Deepak Chopra The Seven Spiritual Laws of Success

10. Hidden Journey – Andrew Harvey

11. Useful Resources:

a Sufis – Their Saints and Shrines. John Subhan

b Buddhism for Beginners

c Eastern Philosophy for Beginners

12. Siddharta – Hermann Hesse

HELP & RESOURCES

Finding help for your emotional issues

So where to get help?

You have to find your own way. The Internet has many resources. They are free. Listen to the Internet talks of famous teachers such as Ajahn Brahm, Eckhart Tolle, and Jon Kabat-Zinn. Buy their books. You will find that as your interest develops you will discover all sorts of resources by yourself.

See A Professional:

The purpose of this section of the book is to promote a way of looking at problems and looking at life. Before proceeding further, **please note that if you have severe anxiety or depression problems, please see a doctor**. The advice given here is not a substitute for standard intervention by the medical profession.

An interesting fact: **NICE Guidelines on Mindfulness based CBT (Cognitive Based Therapy).** In 2008, in their guidance, the UK National Institute for Clinical Excellence acknowledged 'Mindfulness' therapy as a valid approach to anxiety and depression.

However because mindfulness practices have not come from the orthodox medical establishment but from Buddhist thought and practice, the NHS does not have such things as mindfulness counselors. However there appear to be some NHS endorsed websites offering Mindfulness Training programs.

Books and the Internet:

Ajahn Brahm. Buy his book - Open the Door of Your Heart. This is available in the UK as Who Ordered This Truckload Of Dung. It is a book of 108 stories from life. The story called 'This too shall pass' and 'The Anger Eating Demon' are exceptionally pertinent to the issue of dealing with difficult emotions. 'Four Ways of Letting Go' is an exceptional YouTube talk. It has more than 500,000 hits. There are over 50 other YouTube talks, all good. Ajahn's jokes and teaching stories really endear him to his audience. I understand there are some 1000 recorded Ajahn Brahm talks.

I recommend you listen to these wonderful hour long talks by Ajahn Brahm:

1) The Pursuit of Happiness   11.5.2013
2) Success Without Stress   1.3.2012
3) Wanting for Nothing   6.11.2012
4) The Meaning of Life - Peace of Mind 24.1.2009
5) Peace is the Highest Happiness   19.6.2008
6) The Secret   3.4.2008
7) Talk your way to Happiness   11.2.2007

Eckhart Tolle. Buy his book The Power of Now. This is one of the most famous spiritual books of all time. It has a sequel. Practicing the Power of Now. You can also watch him speak on You Tube and via his TV channel.

Other YouTube Recommendations:
Mindfulness with Jon Kabat Zinn - His 2007 talk to Google staff.

Be your own therapist-Ven. Robina Courtin - Talk to Google staff in 2008.

Transforming Problems - Thubten Chodron.

Awakening Compassion - Pema Chodron- 16 sequential half hour talks.

The material in this book on letting go and dealing with difficult emotions arose from my effort to summarise some aspects of the teaching of Ajahn Brahm based on his YouTube talks. If they stimulate the reader's interest then they have achieved their purpose.

This is plenty to go on!

Good Luck with this.

BIBLIOGRAPHY

Autobiography of a Yogi. S.l.: Floating Press, 2008. Print.

Bennett, John G. *Witness: The Autobiography of John G. Bennett.* London: Turnstone Books, 19751974. Print.

Brunton, Paul. *A Search in Secret India,.* New York: E.P. Dutton & Co., inc., 1935. Print.

Brunton, Paul. *A Search in Secret Egypt.* S.l.: s.n.], 1958. Print.

Chopra, Deepak. *The Seven Spiritual Laws of Success: A Practical Guide to the Fulfillment of your Dreams.* San Rafael, Calif.: Amber-Allen Pub. :, 1994. Print.

Craig, Mary. *His Holiness the Dalai Lama: In My Own Words.* London: Hodder & Stoughton, 2001. Print.

Gaffney, Patrick, and Andrew Harvey. *The Tibetan Book of Living and Dying.* San Francisco, Calif.: Harper San Francisco, 1992. Print.

Gibran, Kahlil. *The Prophet.* New York: Knopf, 19521951. Print.

Gurdjieff, Georges Ivanovitch, and A. R. Orage. *Meetings with Remarkable Men.* New York: E.P. Dutton, 1969. Print.

Harvey, Andrew. *Hidden Journey: A Spiritual Awakening.* New York: Holt, 1991. Print.

Kornfield, Jack. *Living Buddhist Masters.* Santa Cruz, CA: Unity Press, 1977. Print.

Krishnamurti, J., and Mary Lutyens. *Freedom from the Known,*. London: Gollancz, 1969. Print.

Living with the Himalayan Masters: Spiritual Experiences of Swami Rama. Honesdale, Pa.: Himalayan International Institute of Yoga Sciences & Philosophy, 1978. Print.

Needleman, Jacob. *Lost Christianity.* Garden City, N.Y.: Doubleday, 1980. Print.

Newton, Michael. *Journey of Souls: Case Studies of Life Between Lives.* St. Paul, Minn.: Llewellyn, 1994. Print.

Peters, Fritz. *Boyhood with Gurdjieff ; Gurdjieff Remembered ; Balanced Man.* Oregon House, Calif.: Bardic Press, 2005. Print.

Svoboda, Robert. *Aghora: at the Left Hand of God.* Albuquerque, N.M.: Brotherhood of Life, Inc., 1986. Print.

Svoboda, Robert. *Aghora II: Kundalini.* Albuquerque, N.M.: Brotherhood of Life, 1993. Print.

Svoboda, Robert. *The Greatness of Saturn.* Tulsa, OK: Sadhana Publications :, 1997. Print.

Svoboda, Robert. *Aghora III: the Law of Karma.* Albuquerque: Brotherhood of Life ;, 1998. Print.

The Four Noble Truths. Hertfordshire, England: Amaravati Publications, 1992. Print.

The Mind and The Way: Buddhist Reflections on Life. Boston, Mass.: Wisdom Publications, 1995. Print.

The Song of God: Bhagavad-Gita - Gita. Phoenix House: New American Library ;, 1959. Print.

Tolle, Eckhart. *The Power of Now: A Guide to Spiritual Enlightenment.* Novato, Calif.: New World Library, 1999. Print.

Uspenskiĭ, P. D.. *In Search of the Miraculous; Fragments of an Unknown Teaching.*. [1st ed. New York: Harcourt, Brace, 1949. Print.

Uspenskiĭ, P. D.. *The Psychology of Man's Possible Evolution.* 2d ed. New York: Knopf; [distributed by Random House], 1974. Print.

Walker, Benjamin. *Masks of the Soul: The Facts Behind Reincarnation.* Wellingborough, Northamptonshire: Aquarian Press, 1981. Print.

Weiss, Brian L.. *Many Lives, Many Masters.* New York: Simon & Schuster, 1988. Print.

Who Ordered This Truckload of Dung?: Inspiring Stories for Welcoming Life's Difficulties. Boston: Wisdom Publications, 2005. Print.

Williams, Lisa. *The Survival of the Soul.* Carlsbad, Calif.: Hay House, 2011. Print

Made in the USA
San Bernardino, CA
26 November 2014